FOUR DESERT FATHERS

Pambo, Evagrius, Macarius of Egypt, and Macarius of Alexandria

T0338975

ST VLADIMIR'S SEMINARY PRESS
Popular Patristics Series
Number 27

The Popular Patristics Series published by St Vladimir's Seminary Press provides readable and accurate translations of a broad range of early Christian literature to a wide audience—from students of Christian history to lay Christians reading for spiritual benefit. Recognized scholars in their fields provide short but comprehensive and clear introductions to the material. The texts include classics of Christian literature, thematic volumes, collections of homilies, letters on spiritual counsel, and poetical works from a variety of geographical contexts and historical backgrounds. The mission of the series is to mine the riches of the early Church and to make these treasures available to all.

Series Editor
BOGDAN BUCUR

Associate Editor
IGNATIUS GREEN

* * *

Series Editor
1999–2020
JOHN BEHR

FOUR DESERT FATHERS

Pambo, Evagrius, Macarius of Egypt, and Macarius of Alexandria

Coptic Texts Relating to the *Lausiac History* of Palladius

Translated, with Introductions, by

TIM VIVIAN

With the Assistance of ROWAN A. GREER

Preface by ADALBERT DE VOGÜÉ, OSB

ST VLADIMIR'S SEMINARY PRESS
CRESTWOOD, NEW YORK
2004

Library of Congress Cataloging-in-Publication Data

De Historia Lausica, quanam sit huius ad Monachorum Aegyptiorum historiam scribendam utilitas. English.

Four desert fathers : Pambo, Evagrius, Macarius of Egypt, and Macarius of Alexandria : coptic texts relating to the lausiac history of Palladius / translated, with introductions by Tim Vivian ; with the assistance of Rowan A. Greer ; preface by Adalbert de Vog.

      p.   cm. — (St. Vladimir's Seminary Press "popular patristics" series)
      Includes bibliographical references and index.
      ISBN 0–88141–256–2 (alk. paper)
      1. Desert Fathers—Biography.   2. Christian biography—Egypt.
3. Spiritual Life—Christianity.   4. Desert Fathers—Quotations.   I. Vivian,
Tim.   II. Greer, Rowan A..   III. Title.   IV. Series.

BR1705.A2D4 2004
270.2'092'2—dc22

2004020367

PRINTED IN THE UNITED STATES OF AMERICA

In a way, each one judges himself merely by what he does. Does, not says. Yet let us not completely dismiss words. They do have meaning. They are related to action. They spring from action and they prepare for it, they clarify it, they direct it.

—Thomas Merton
Turning Toward the World

I know that . . . I have mentioned many people and events that you know little of, that you may in fact know nothing of, for they have not come down in the historical record. They are not part of the received truth. It is important that you hear them, however. . . .

—Russell Banks
Cloudsplitter

To

Gabriel Bunge, OSB

Adalbert de Vogüé, OSB

Contents

Foreword

We can be grateful to the author for his judicious selection and careful editing of this series of Coptic texts about some of the great fourth-century Egyptian hermits. Some years ago, Gabriel Bunge and I published in French the four Coptic fragments from the *Lausiac History* that make up the first of these two volumes. I am therefore particularly pleased to find that they are accompanied in the second volume by another three documents about the most famous of these four hermits: Macarius the Egyptian, also known as Macarius the Great.

Pambo, Evagrius, and two abbas named Macarius—the order is not the same as that of Palladius, who put Evagrius after the two Macarii, nor does it correspond to the chronological order of these early monks, but it does have the considerable advantage of taking us in turn to each of the main centres where Egyptian eremiticism developed successively during the fourth century. We start at Nitria, where Pambo lived, then move on to Kellia, the home of Evagrius, and finally to Scetis, where both Macarii lived. In a way, our itinerary from Nitria to Kellia and on to Scetis takes us through the history of monasticism, from the foundation of Nitria by Amoun to the four presbyteral churches of Scetis familiar to Cassian via the anchorite colony of Kellia, founded from Nitria, of which the *Historia Monachorum* has left us such a delightful picture.

Palladius tells us that three of the four great monks he has described for us, Pambo and the two Macarii, were priests, whereas Evagrius was a deacon when he came to the desert and remained such, despite the attempts to raise him to the episcopate. It is true that the Coptic text of the *Lausiac History* omits the Greek phrase which tells us that Macarius the Great was a priest, but the *Life* of this saint by Serapion of Thmuis makes good this lacuna by reporting the ordination of Macarius prior to his entering monastic life.

So, then, we have these four famous hermits, all in major orders and yet all enamoured of solitude. Apart from these general similarities, however, they have little else in common. The contrast between the first two is striking. What could be more different from Pambo, a manual worker who avoided speech, than Evagrius, a gifted intellectual who used his fingers only to write and who spent much of his time teaching? As for the two Macarii, Macarius the Egyptian seems hardly ever to have left Scetis, where he had a constant stream of visitors, whereas Macarius of Alexandria had cells in various places and often journeyed from one to the other.

There is also a profound difference between the first two accounts, from which the marvellous is virtually absent, and the last two, where it abounds. Neither Pambo nor Evagrius worked any miracles. Evagrius did converse with an angel while he was still a deacon in Constantinople, and later he was beaten by demons, three of whom also came to debate with him, but we do not see him actually working any miracles. It is not Evagrius, but one of his visitors, who is supplied with two warm loaves from some mysterious source every day. As for Evagrius himself, there is nothing marvellous about the purse he found on his path one day, even if he suspected that a demon may have put it there to try him.

In contrast, both Abba Macarius the Egyptian and Abba Macarius of Alexandria work sensational wonders. One of them raises someone from the dead, no less; the other is given milk by an antelope, is obeyed by a hyena whose cubs he has healed, roots to the spot a she-camel that was about to carry away some stolen objects, and restores as well the health of numerous human beings. Yet the intention of Palladius is not to astound his reader with marvellous tales. When he recounts a resurrection brought about by Macarius the Great, it is in order to admire the indifference to human glory shown by the saint in these circumstances. When he also tells us that the same Macarius restored the human appearance of a woman who had been changed into a mare, it is to extract a very lowly and practical moral: Sunday Mass must not be missed. As for the bulimic young man who was about to die, his ills resulted from the lack of charity of his parents. Each of these miracles carries a religious and moral lesson, which extends the teaching and example given by the saint.

It is true that the spiritual significance of the marvellous deeds recounted is sometimes less obvious. This is particularly true of three miracles worked by Macarius of Alexandria at the end of the biography: a cup broken on the altar is repaired, sand is turned into an edible gruel, and during a drought there is a sudden, torrential downpour, which then stops just as suddenly. However, the last two wonders had the effect of converting the onlookers, who had come to see Macarius, their former colleague, and who realised that despite his homely conversation he was no longer the same as before but had given himself entirely to the Lord, whom they themselves began to serve. As for the people of Alexandria who witnessed the miracle of the rain and the numerous healings brought about by the saint, "many of them were saved"—an allusion to the effects of grace and of conversion obtained as a result of this great monk's visit to the capital, which recalls that of Pambo described earlier and, above all, that of Antony at the time of the Arian dispute.

Paradoxically, the good of their neighbour is the constant concern of these great solitaries. The words of Macarius of Egypt highlight the beneficial or harmful impact of words spoken to others. They teach that one must not judge, they urge kindness to sinners and compassion for those who are tempted. Pambo gives the fruits of his labour to the poor and also gives the poor the offerings of his admirers, for which he has no use himself. This practical love of neighbour gives meaning to the characteristic monastic desire to belong entirely to God, which is constantly reaffirmed in these stories. "No human friendships," teaches Macarius the Great: it is God's company that must be sought. Restricted to limited and necessary contacts, the heart opens to a divine love that embraces all people.

It is in this perspective that the ceaseless search for solitude and silence takes place. "Remain in your cell" is a basic teaching. There, the monk tirelessly listens to the word of God, not only by reading the Bible, but by constantly "meditating" on it, by reciting the text by heart. This listening to the divine voice goes on during walking, manual work, and every other occupation and leads to the response of prayer. Every day Evagrius punctuated his meditation with a thousand prayers. We can see how such a dialogue with God would inspire a love of silence. Anyone engaged in it cannot fail to "flee" from human chatter, as Macarius used to say.

However, curiously enough, towards the end of the "Virtues" of Macarius, a community orientation emerges, which at first sight seems to diverge from the general "anachoretic" tendency. The parable of the straying sheep, whose lamb is snatched by a wolf, suggests that solitaries should band together. We should not be too hasty to interpret this as a call to cenobitism, however. In three short chapters, which have not come down to us in Coptic, the *Lausiac History* describes the unhappy hermits of Scetis, who failed to maintain a proper sense of ecclesial communion and necessary human relationships. The solitary life inevitably involves some degree of contact with others. Macarius' word may refer to this minimal social structure.

Another tendency which foreshadows the practice of future centuries is that of the fairly numerous "Virtues" in which Macarius recommends invoking the name of Jesus. But even this advice is given less frequently than calls to humility. This virtue, the only one which radically distinguishes between the holy man and the Devil, is not only the main theme of the teaching of Macarius, it is also reflected by several episodes in his life. Sometimes he puts up with insults and harsh treatment, sometimes he honours those who insult him, sometimes he refuses to let people kiss his hands, and sometimes he takes the smaller share of the palms he has gathered, leaving the bigger share for someone else. He repeatedly demonstrates his humility, not to mention the detachment and indifference to profit that he shows in the last situation.

In Cassian, this virtue of humility, which makes one resemble Christ, was soon to become the heart of the cenobitic doctrine professed by Pinuphius, which in turn was to constitute the core of the Rules of the Master and of Saint Benedict. A modern Benedictine can only rejoice to find that it is already acclaimed in this way in the *Sayings* and *Virtues* of Macarius the Great.

Another useful lesson given in these pages is that of bodily asceticism, which has, alas, so strangely disappeared from modern monasticism, as from Christianity as a whole. It is good to learn that Macarius of Alexandria usually ate only once a week and that the Great Macarius of Egypt made up for every glass of wine he had been forced to consume by abstaining from water, that he condemned all satiety, even of bread and water, and taught that "manual work is nothing without ascesis." When Macarius recalled with great moderation that "it is fitting to fast until the ninth hour," this is simply a forerunner to the directions of Benedict's Rule, which have lost nothing of their importance today.

In this book, Tim Vivian transmits to us this ever-relevant message of the early monks. Once more, we would like to thank him for doing so.

Adalbert de Vogüé
La Pierre-qui-Vire

translated by an Irish hermit

Preface

Ten years ago Gabriel Bunge and Adalbert de Vogüé published a groundbreaking work, based on previously published articles by the two authors, *Quatre ermites égyptiens: d'après les fragments coptes de l'Histoire Lausiaque* (Spiritualité Orientale 60; Bégrolles-en-Mauges: Bellefontaine, 1994). In this volume they offer a French translation of four monastic *Lives*, preserved in Coptic (the Coptic Palladiana), that are clearly related to the Greek *Lausiac History* of Palladius but that also differ dramatically from the same *Lives* in the Greek *History*. The four are: Pambo, Evagrius, Macarius of Egypt (Macarius the Great), and Macarius of Alexandria. Vogüé provides translations based on much improved texts, while Bunge, in a thorough introduction, discusses the relationship between the Coptic *Lives* and the *Lausiac History* and argues for their importance as primary documents witnessing to the early years of Egyptian monasticism.

The paired volumes offered here—*Four Desert Fathers* and *Saint Macarius the Spiritbearer*—began as an effort to bring the fruits of Bunge and Vogüé's work to a wider audience, to offer English translations of the four Coptic *Lives* and provide an introduction to them that, in part, distills the work of Bunge and Vogüé and makes these works more accessible to a modern audience. *Four Desert Fathers* thus offers translations of these four Coptic *Lives*, preceded by an Introduction. The four were originally published separately in different form in the *Coptic Church Review*; I wish to thank the *Review* and its editor, Rodolph Yanney, M.D., for ceding

17

the copyright to me and thus making them available for publication in this volume.

As my work progressed on *Four Desert Fathers*, I saw that three other Coptic texts relating to Saint Macarius the Great also deserved to be translated into English and should form a separate volume: as supplements to the Coptic Palladiana, but also as important documents in their own right. These three texts are *The Sayings of Saint Macarius*, *The Virtues of Saint Macarius* (for which I supply corrections to the text edited by Amélineau), and *The Life of Saint Macarius of Scetis*. Translations of these three texts thus appear as the second volume, *Saint Macarius the Spiritbearer*, which has its own Introduction. The *Sayings* appeared in a different form in *Cistercian Studies Quarterly* and selections of the *Virtues* appeared in *Hallel*; I wish to thank the editors of those journals, Fr Charles Cummings, OCSO, and Fr Ciarán Ó Sabhaois, OCSO, respectively, for their permission to reprint.

During the long and enjoyable gestation of this work, I have had help and encouragement from a number of people. I wish especially to thank William Harmless, S.J. for reading early drafts of each chapter, for his numerous suggestions, and above all for his support and encouragement. I wish to thank Monica Blanchard for her editorial assistance. My thanks to Rowan A. Greer for translating the Syriac text for Appendix II. Apostolos Athanassakis, Augustine Casiday, William Harmless, S.J., Dar Brooks Hedstrom, Maged Mikhail, Birger Pearson, Mark Sheridan, OSB, and Terry Wilfong helped with specific questions and each of them has my thanks. I wish to thank Jeffrey Russell for reading early drafts of the manuscript and offering numerous suggestions for improvement, and especially Adalbert de Vogüé, OSB, for reading the completed manuscript. Père Vogüé also graciously agreed to write a foreword. I wish to thank Fr John Behr, editor of the Popular Patristics series at Saint Vladimir's Seminary Press, for reading the manuscript and making helpful suggestions.

Finally, I wish to thank my family for their love and support: Miriam, Meredith, John, and David. And Amma Joyce, who is always asking what I'm working on.

The Feast of Saint Mary Magdalene, 2003

Tim Vivian
Bakersfield, California

Abbreviations

ACW   Ancient Christian Writers (New York: Paulist Press)

Am   É. Amélineau, *Histoire des monastères de la Basse-Égypte* (Annales du Musée Guimet, 25; Paris: Leroux, 1894)

AP   *Apophthegmata Patrum* (*Sayings of the Fathers*). [Alphabetical AP may be found in PG 65.71–440]

Butler   *The Lausiac History of Palladius*, ed. and trans. Cuthbert Butler (2 vols.; Cambridge: Cambridge UP, 1898 and 1904)

BV   Gabriel Bunge and Adalbert de Vogüé, *Quatre ermites égyptiens: d'après les fragments coptes de l'*Histoire Lausiaque (Spiritualité Orientale 60; Bégrolles-en-Mauges: Bellefontaine, 1994)

Chaîne   M. Chaîne, "La double recension de l'*Histoire Lausique* dans la version copte," *Revue de l'orient chrétien*, 25 (1925–26): 232–75

Crum   Walter Ewing Crum, *A Coptic Dictionary* (Oxford: Clarendon, 1939)

EH   *Ecclesiastical History* (by Eusebius, Rufinus, Socrates or Sozomen)

Evelyn White   Hugh G. Evelyn White, ed. by Walter Hauser, *The Monasteries of the Wâdi 'n Natrûn*, 3 vols. (New York: Metropolitan Museum of Art, 1926–1933 [repr. Arno Press: New York, 1973]). Part I: *New Coptic Texts from the Monastery of Saint Macarius*, Part II: *The History of the Monasteries of Nitria and Scetis*, Part III: *The Architecture and Archaeology*

Gk   Greek

Lampe   G. W. H. Lampe, *A Patristic Greek Lexicon* (Oxford: Clarendon, 1961)

LH	Palladius, *Lausiac History*
LSJ	Henry George Liddell and Robert Scott, rev. Henry Stuart Jones, *A Greek English Lexicon* (Oxford: Clarendon, 1968)
LXX	The Septuagint; *Septuaginta*, ed. Alfred Rahlfs (Stuttgart: Deutsche Bibelstiftung Stuttgart, 1935)
Meyer	*Palladius: The Lausiac History*, trans. Robert T. Meyer (New York: Newman Press, 1964)
PG	Patrologia Graeca
Ramsey	*John Cassian: The Conferences*, trans. by Boniface Ramsey (Mahwah, NJ: Paulist Press, 1997)
Regnault	Lucien Regnault, *Les Sentences des Pères du désert: Troisieme recueil et tables* (Solesmes, 1976)
Russell	*The Lives of the Desert Fathers: The Historia Monachorum in Aegypto*, trans. by Norman Russell (Kalamazoo: Cistercian, 1981)
SC	Sources chrétiennes (Paris: Cerf)
Vogüé	Adalbert de Vogüé, *Quatre ermites égyptiens: d'après les fragments coptes de* l'Histoire Lausiaque (Spiritualite Orientalé 60; Bégrolles-en-Mauges: Bellefontaine, 1994)
Ward	Benedicta Ward, trans., *The Sayings of the Desert Fathers: The Alphabetical Collection* (rev. ed.; Kalamazoo: Cistercian, 1984)

Biblical quotations are from the RSV and NRSV.

As noted at the beginning of each translation from the Coptic text, italics are used to indicate portions lacking in the Greek *LH*.

FOUR DESERT FATHERS

Introduction

Taking God: The Anthropomorphite Controversy

The four desert Fathers who give their names to this volume—
Pambo, Evagrius, Macarius of Egypt, and Macarius of Alexandria—
were well known in late antiquity but were most famous, perhaps,
because of their Lives recounted by the monk (and later bishop) Palladius in his *Lausiac History*. The *Lausiac History*, however, is not a
straightforward historical source; theological and spiritual issues,
indeed arguments and bitter fisticuffs, have seemingly shaped its
form and contents. The most important of these issues vis-à-vis the
four Lives offered here were Origenism and the Anthropomorphite
controversy. Before we look at Palladius and Evagrius, Origenism,
the spiritual and theological ramifications of the Anthropomorphite
controversy, and their subsequent effect on the *Lausiac History* and
the four Coptic Lives of this volume, we should first walk through
the terrain of the controversy itself at the very end of the fourth century. To do so, however, we need guides, and this presents us with an
immediate problem: all the guides we rely on in this territory are
biased; we have maps, but maps require interpretation and a knowledge of the landscape. With that in mind, here is a sketch of what
happened some 1600 years ago in Alexandria and some of the
monastic communities of Lower Egypt.

The Church historian Socrates (380–450) has given one of the
fullest—though hardly unbiased—accounts.[1] Socrates, interest-

---

[1] See Socrates *EH* 6.7; the translation used below is that of A. C. Zenos in volume
two of *The Nicene and Post-Nicene Fathers*, second series (Grand Rapids, MI: Eerd-
mans, 1979), 142–144. See also Sozomen *EH* 8.12.

ingly, begins with the theological issues: "whether God is a corporeal existence, and has the form of man; or whether he is incorporeal, and without human or, generally speaking, any other bodily shape." Immediately showing his bias, Socrates declares that "the more simple ascetics asserted that God is corporeal, and has a human figure" while "most others condemn" that belief. In the forefront of this latter, theologically astute, multitude (says Socrates) stood no less a figure than Theophilus, bishop of Alexandria, who "inveighed against those who attributed to God a human form." According to John Cassian, who had been in Egypt at the time of the Anthropomorphite controversy, Theophilus made his position clear in his Easter letter of 399.[2] Socrates rather blandly says that when the Egyptian monks learned of Theophilus' position, "they left their monasteries and came to Alexandria." Cassian puts things more dramatically: according to him, "all . . . the monks . . . throughout . . . Egypt" received Theophilus' letter "with such great bitterness" that the "vast majority of elders" decided that the bishop "should be abominated" and declared a heretic.[3]

The sources then agree that Theophilus, threatened by throngs of monks, did an about-face: "In seeing you," he diplomatically— and ambiguously—told the monks, "I behold the face of God." The monks, placated, accepted Theophilus' "apology," but demanded that he "anathematize Origen's books," for "some drawing arguments from them oppose themselves to our opinion."[4] Theophilus, although an admirer of Origen, the great third-century Alexandrian theologian, played the politician and avowed his disapproval of the Alexandrian's writings and so the monks left, appeased. Socrates says that matters would have ended here had not ecclesiastical politics taken over. Theophilus became embroiled in a bitter dispute with the four Tall Brothers, well-known monastic and episcopal

[2]Cassian *Conferences* 10.2.
[3]Cassian *Conferences* 10.2.2; *John Cassian: The Conferences*, translated by Boniface Ramsey, O.P. (New York/Mahwah: Paulist Press, 1997), 371.
[4]Socrates *EH* 6.7.

leaders. They, influenced by Origen, maintained that God was incorporeal. Theophilus, Socrates says, held the same theological position but in order to wreak vengeance on the brothers, attacked their position and polarized the monks even further: "A division being thus made, both parties branded each other as impious"; the "corporealists" labeled their opponents "Origenists" while the "incorporealists" vilified their opposites as "Anthropomorphites." Theophilus convened a synod in 400 to effect the condemnation of Origen and to excommunicate the Origenist monks, the Tall Brothers. In the spring of 400, with soldiers and "a drunken rabble," he attacked Nitria at night and drove the followers of Origen, perhaps three hundred monks, out of Egypt.[5] Many of the monks fled to Constantinople; this flight would unintentionally help bring down that city's bishop, John Chrysostom, and lead to his exile and death.

Cassian gives a decidedly one-sided view of matters but through his depiction of the Anthropomorphite monk Serapion puts a human face on this ancient theological and ecclesiastical dispute. Serapion, in Cassian's view, was ignorant and "ensnared in error"; when this simple monk was convinced of the foolishness of his position, "he realized that the anthropomorphic image of the Godhead which he had always pictured to himself while praying had been banished from his heart." With this realization, "he suddenly broke into the bitterest tears and heavy sobbing." Throwing himself to the ground, with a loud groan he cried out, "Woe is me, wretch that I am! They have taken my God from me, and I have no one to lay hold of, nor do I know whom I should adore or address."[6] The Anthropomorphite controversy, then, was—at least in part—about how one "takes" or understands God. As Serapion's heartbreaking cry

[5]Palladius *Dialogue* 7; *Dialogus de vita S. Joannis Chrysostomi*, ed. P. R. Coleman-Norton (Cambridge: Cambridge UP, 1928), 39. Socrates *EH* 6.7. See A. Guillaumont, *Les "Kephalaia Gnostica" d'Évagre le Pontique et l'histoire de l'origénisme chez les Grecs et chez les Syriens*, Patristica Sorboniensia 5 (Paris, 1962), 62–64. Guillaumont, 64 n. 72, following Butler (2.244), believes that Palladius left Nitria in 399, thus before the condemnation of and attack upon the Origenist monks.

[6]Cassian *Conferences* 10.3.4–5; Ramsey, trans., 372–373.

makes clear, a loser in the controversy could feel that his God had
been taken from him. Unfortunately, the Anthropomorphite controversy was like a cluster bomb dropped in a populated area: after
its initial explosion it continued to wreak long-term mayhem and
destruction: on monks like Serapion, on the "Origenists" forced to
flee Egypt, on John Chrysostom, on the posthumous reputations of
Origen and Evagrius. Palladius may have been driven from Egypt
because of the controversy, and subsequent anti-Origenism may
have helped determine the final form of his *Lausiac History*.

Palladius (363–364 to before 431)

Palladius was born in Galatia fifty years after the Peace of the
Church;[7] little is known of his early life, though he appears to have
had a good classical education. Around 386 he became a monk and
in 390 travelled to Egypt: first to Alexandria, then to Nitria, and then
on to Kellia, where he lived for nine years.[8] He may have been driven
from Egypt in 399 during the persecution of the Origenist monks by
Theophilus, the patriarch of Alexandria; he went to Constantinople,
where he became the friend and defender of its besieged patriarch,
John Chrysostom. Around 400 he became bishop of Helenopolis in
Bithynia. When Chrysostom was exiled by the emperor, Palladius
defended him at Rome before Pope Innocent I. When he returned
to Constantinople in 406, he was banished to Egypt; allowed
back, he returned home to Galatia, where he became bishop of
Aspuna.[9] Around 420 he wrote the *Lausiac History* (dedicated to the

[7]In *Lausiac History* (hereafter *LH*) 35.5, Palladius tells John of Lycopolis that he
is "a stranger come from Galatia."

[8]For Palladius' account of his experiences, see *LH* 1–7; see C. H. Turner, "Palladiana II: The Lausiac History. Questions of History," *Journal of Theological Studies* 22
(1921): 21–35 and 138–55.

[9]According to Socrates *EH* 7.36, Palladius was "transferred" from Helenopolis to
Aspuna; we have this information because Socrates, in defending translations of bishops from one see to another, cites Palladius' case as one among many.

emperor's chamberlain, Lausus; hence its name) and probably died before 431.[10]

Palladius and Evagrius

One eminent scholar has declared, correctly, that the *Lausiac History* is "a work written in the spirit of Evagrius."[11] Certainly Evagrius holds an exalted place in the *History*: he is almost always "blessed Evagrius" or, like Saints Peter and Paul, he is joined at the canonical hip with (tellingly) Ammonius, the Origenist leader of the Tall Brothers.[12] This close association must have been widely known throughout the desert: when Palladius goes to visit John of Lycopolis, John says (drily? matter-of-factly? humorously?), "I presume that you are from Evagrius' community [*sunodias*]." Palladius "admits" (*hōmologēsa*) that he "belongs to Evagrius' group [*hetaireias*]."[13] Undoubtedly, the feelings between Palladius and Evagrius were mutual: Palladius venerates Evagrius as "my teacher," and Evagrius reciprocates by embracing Palladius as his "brother." The historian Socrates agrees with Palladius, terming him a "disciple of Evagrius."[14]

---

[10]On the thought and spirituality of the *Lausiac History*, see Nicolas Molinier, *Ascèse, contemplation et ministère d'après l'Histoire Lausiaque de Pallade d'Hélénopolis* (Spiritualité Orientale 64; Bégrolles-en-Mauges: Bellefontaine, 1995).

[11]See René Draguet, "L'Histoire Lausiaque, une oeuvre écrite dans l'esprit d'Évagre," *Revue d'Histoire Ecclésiastique* 41 (1946): 321–364; 42: 5–49. Jeremy Driscoll, in agreeing with this assessment, sees Evagrius as part of the mainstream of early Egyptian monasticism and nuances Draguet's phrase: "Thus, 'a work in the spirit of Evagrius' needs to mean that we have to do here not just with the spirit of one peculiar innovator but rather with the tradition that he represents." See Driscoll, "Evagrius and Paphnutius on the causes for abandonment by God," *Studia Monastica* 39.2 (1997): 259–86, at 261.

[12]"Blessed": *LH* 11.1, 35.3, 47.3, 86.1; "Saints Ammonius and Evagrius": *LH* 24.2. Gabriel Bunge, "Évagre le Pontique et les deux Macaires," *Irénikon* 56 (1983): 215–27, 323–60, has observed, 324, that Palladius uses more honorific titles for Evagrius than for Macarius of Alexandria.

[13]*LH* 35.5.

[14]*LH* 23.1 (Meyer, 81), Evagrius *Epistle* 51.1, and Socrates *EH* 4.23.

As Palladius himself says about Evagrius in the Coptic fragment of the *Life of Evagrius*, "Indeed, it was also he who taught me the way of life in Christ and he who helped me understand Holy Scripture . . . for the whole time I was in that monastic community I was with him, each of us living enclosed and apart. I was by his side Saturday night and during the day on Sunday." This testimony survives only in Coptic, and may have been excised from the Greek manuscripts of the *Lausiac History*. The discipleship, or friendship, or brotherhood of Palladius with Evagrius, however we term it, was to get Palladius in trouble during his lifetime and, after his death, cause his *History* the mutilation of censorship and expurgation. Why should this have been so? Who was Evagrius, and why did he theologically contaminate Palladius and his writing?

Evagrius (345–399)

According to Palladius (*LH* 38), Evagrius was from Pontus, born in 345 or 346. Made a reader by Basil of Caesarea and ordained a deacon by Gregory of Nazianzus, Evagrius moved in the highest ecclesiastical circles; in 381 he accompanied Gregory to the Synod of Constantinople.[15] An (apparently unconsummated) indiscretion with a highly-placed lady caused him quickly to flee Constantinople and sail for the Holy Land, where the renowned monastic patroness Melania welcomed him. Evagrius, however, had not really changed his ways; in *Lausiac History* 38.8, Palladius says that the Devil "hardened his heart" and that Evagrius was "vainglorious," while the Coptic *Life* reports that he was somewhat of a dandy, often changing his clothes. After he was struck with a God-given illness, Melania got him to embrace the monastic life and leave for Egypt, probably in 383. He lived in Nitria for two or three years, then came to Kellia in

[15]On the "historical and theological links" between Evagrius and the Cappadocians, see Elizabeth A. Clark, *The Origenist Controversy: The Cultural Construction of an Early Christian Debate* (Princeton: Princeton UP, 1992), 60–61.

384–85, where he became a disciple of Macarius of Alexandria and apparently knew Macarius of Egypt.[16] Here he lived the rest of his life "in truly apostolic fashion," dying in 399, just before the Origenist storm—or cataclysm—swept over the monastic settlements of Lower Egypt, dividing communities and driving hundreds of monks, including Palladius, Ammonius, and the Tall Brothers, into exile. Hugh G. Evelyn White considered Evagrius' death a *felix opportunitas mortis* (he died at an opportune time).[17] One wonders if some of Evagrius' friends and disciples, on their way out of Egypt and into bitter exile, did not stop at his grave and envy him for the peace they believed he most surely had obtained in the kingdom of God. Such peace, unfortunately, was not to attach to his posthumous name on earth. Unlike the great Origen, he was not so much calumnied as just "disappeared." Despite this disappearance—and censorship and expurgation—Evagrius continued to be prized in antiquity for his keen ascetic insights, and the past twenty to thirty years have witnessed a renewed appreciation of his writings.

Evagrius and the Anthropomorphite and Origenist Controversies

Two hundred years after his death, Evagrius' cell at Kellia was still considered by some to be haunted by an evil demon that had led "Evagrius astray, alienating him from the true faith, and it filled his

---

[16]*Historia Monachorum* (Latin) 27; see also Evagrius *Praktikos* 93. Socrates says that Evagrius was a disciple of both Macarii—Macarius of Egypt (the Great) and Macarius of Alexandria. The former, however, lived in Scetis, while the latter was at Kellia. Evagrius does say, *Capita practica ad Anatolium* (PG 40.1220), that he was at Scetis, but Evelyn White, 2.84–86, suggests that "Scetis" is a generic term for the three monastic communities of lower Egypt: Nitria, Kellia, and Scetis (Wadi al-Natrun). According to Palladius *LH* 18.10, Macarius the Alexandrian had cells in several places: in the Great Desert, in Libya, at Kellia, and at Nitria. On Evagrius and the two Macarii, see Antoine Guillaumont, "Le problème des deux Macaires dans les *Apophthegmata Patrum*," Irénikon 48 (1975): 41–59, and Bunge, "Évagre le Pontique et les deux Macaires."

[17]Evelyn White, 2.86.

mind with abominable teachings." A brother "from foreign parts" came to Kellia and asked to stay in Evagrius' cell. Possibly mindful of the saying of Saint Macarius of Egypt, "Do not sleep in the cell of a brother who has a bad reputation,"[18] the priest tried to dissuade him, but the brother insisted. The first week he stayed there without incident, but the second week he failed to appear on Sunday; when the priest went to check on him, he found that "the brother had put a rope around his neck and strangled himself."[19] This story undoubtedly circulated in monastic circles as a cautionary tale warning against "Evagrian" tendencies.[20] Other evidence, however, shows that Evagrius' writings were still being requested by monks in Egypt in the seventh and eighth centuries.[21] The *Virtues of Macarius*, assembled after 450, closely link Evagrius with Macarius the Great, one of the most eminent saints of Egypt.[22] In them Evagrius is called "the wise," hardly an epithet applied to someone anathematized.[23] Did the unfortunate "foreign" suicide at Kellia mentioned

[18] *AP* Macarius the Great 29; Ward, 133.

[19] John Moschus *Pratum spirituale* 177; *The Spiritual Meadow of John Moschus*, trans. John Wortley (Kalamazoo: Cistercian, 1992), 146–147.

[20] This story of Evagrius' demon is a foreshadowing as it were of the condemnation of Origen in the sixth century where Evagrius, not Origen, is the real enemy; see Antoine Guillaumont, *Les "Kephalaia Gnostica"* and Brian E. Daley, "What did 'Origenism' Mean in the Sixth Century?" in *Origeniana Sexta*, ed. Gilles Dorival and Alain Le Bonfluec (Leuven: Peeters, 1995), 627–638.

[21] W. E. Crum, *Coptic Ostraca from the Collections of the Egypt Exploration Fund, the Cairo Museum and Others* (London: Egypt Exploration Fund, 1902), #252 (Coptic, 46; English, 63): " 'I said to [Apa] Anthony that he should get *The Paradise* from Apa John and bring it to me. Otherwise, send the two (books) together. And please send Apa Evagrius.' " For other examples of ancient requests in Egypt for Evagrius' works, see Joseph Muyldermans, "Evagriana Coptica," *Le Muséon* 76 (1963): 271–276, esp. 272–273. Muyldermans believes that these requests were for the *Antirrhetikos* or the *Praktikos*.

[22] For the *Virtues*, see the companion volume to this one, *Saint Macarius the Spiritbearer*. See Bunge, "Évagre le Pontique et les deux Macaires," 346–347. As Bunge says, parts of the *Virtues* are very ancient; the ties between Macarius and Evagrius were undoubtedly forged much earlier than the seventh century (the century in which he believes the *Virtues* were compiled), but it is worth noting that later editors and scribes did not see the need to excise Evagrius from the text.

[23] *Virtues* 69.

above come from Asia Minor or Syria, where Evagrius' works still circulated and where his ascetical teaching was still admired? Was the curse on Evagrius somehow a lingering memory of (some) Egyptian resentment against the earlier foreign (that is, Greek) interloper, a tension hinted at in the *Apophthegmata*?[24] If so, how representative was this resentment?

These questions are ultimately unanswerable, but they are suggestive. In none of the sources concerning the Anthropomorphite-Origenist controversy is Evagrius cast as a villain. Nor does he come on stage as a hero. In fact, he does not appear at all; he simply disappears from the historical record. The *damnatio memoriae* against Evagrius was so complete that both sides in the controversy honored it, though undoubtedly for very different reasons (John Cassian, one of Evagrius' most ardent admirers, never mentions him by name, though his works are suffused with Evagrius' spirit).[25] Our chief sources for this controversy are the Church historian Socrates and the monastic writers Cassian and Palladius, all of whom, to say the least, are biased against the Anthropomorphites and against Theophilus, the archbishop of Alexandria who ultimately took their side.

Scholars have seen two monastic camps: "Hellenic or Hellenized monks whose theology was more intellectual and more speculative than the naïve and literal beliefs of their Egyptian brethren."[26] While this demarcation is suspiciously tidy and accepts the anti-Anthro-

[24]*AP* Evagrius 7. Because of Evagrius' continued good name in Coptic tradition (in the synaxary versions of the *LH* and in the *Virtues of Saint Macarius*), Bunge, "Évagre le Pontique et les deux Macaires," 358 n. 208, wonders whether that tradition remembered him unfavorably or whether he was thought to be implicated in the Anthropomorphite controversy.

[25]To give just one example outside of the *Lausiac History*: in the received Greek text of *AP* Arsenius 5, "someone" asks Arsenius why "we" with our education get nowhere while the uneducated Egyptian peasants acquire virtue. In several recensions, this "someone" is identified as Evagrius who, given the subject, is a likely interlocutor. Antoine Guillaumont, "Les *Kephalaia Gnostika*," 53 n. 20 has noted "the tendency of the Greek to make the name of Evagrius disappear."

[26]Evelyn White, 2.128.

pomorphite biases of the ancient sources, it probably presents a reasonably, though not entirely, accurate picture.[27] The divide between Origenists and anti-Origenists, anti-Anthropomorphites and Anthropomorphites, was not entirely ethnic but also involved social networks, particularly among the Origenists.[28] In *Conference* 10.3, Cassian speaks highly of Paphnutius, a Copt, who opposed Anthropomorphism in Scetis. It is not a coincidence that in that same Conference, Paphnutius calls on a foreigner, "a certain deacon named Photinus" from Cappadocia, who informs the monks that "the Catholic churches throughout the East" interpreted Genesis "spiritually," not in a "lowly" way like the Anthropomorphites.[29]

Evagrius' roots were in Cappadocia, and the Cappadocians were very sympathetic to Origen.[30] Evagrius also had close ties to Melania the Elder. According to our sources, it is to her that he owed his monastic vocation; if that is accurate, then it is reasonable to suppose that without Melania there might not have been Evagrius the "erudite theologian" of monasticism.[31] But Melania, more than

[27]Graham Gould has challenged the traditional picture, "The Image of God and the Anthropomorphite Controversy in Fourth Century Monasticism," in Robert J. Daley, ed., *Origeniana Quinta* (Leuven: University Press, 1992), 549–565.

[28]On this issue see particularly Clark, *The Origenist Controversy*, esp. chaps. 1 and 2. Some of the Origenists—Pambo, Paphnutius—were Copts, while some—Evagrius—were Greeks. The Tall Brothers seem to have been Egyptian; three of their names (Dioscorus, Euthymius, and Eusebius) are Greek, while "Ammonius" is Egyptian in origin.

[29]A non-literal view of God went with a non-literal view of Scripture; see Elizabeth A. Clark, *Reading Renunciation: Asceticism and Scripture in Early Christianity* (Princeton: Princeton UP, 1999), esp. chap. 4, "The Profits and Perils of Figurative Exegesis."

[30]Evagrius undoubtedly first came to know Origen's works through the Cappadocians' selection of the latter's writings known as the *Philocalia*; see Socrates *EH* 4.26, and Guillaumont, *Les "Kephalaia Gnostica,"* 48–50; see also Nicholas Gendle, "Cappadocian Elements in the Mystical Theology of Evagrius Ponticus," *Studia Patristica* 16, 373–384. On Evagrius' intellectual and spiritual connections with Origen, see Francis X. Murphy, "Evagrius Ponticus and Origenism," in Richard Hanson and Henri Crouzel, eds., *Origeniana Tertia* (Rome: Edizioni dell' Ateneo, 1985), 253–269, and Guillaumont, *Les "Kephalaia Gnostica,"* 40–46, 81–123.

[31]The phrase is borrowed from Louis Bouyer, *The Spirituality of the New Testament and the Fathers*, Vol. 1: *A History of Christian Spirituality* (Minneapolis: The Seabury Press, 1963).

being a way-station on Evagrius' vocational journey, has even closer associations with Egypt and Origenism, and thus with the Anthropomorphite controversy.[32] She and Rufinus (345–411)—monk, historian, translator, and befriender of Origen's writings—met in either Rome or Egypt in the 370s; in 373–374 they visited Nitria and there met Pambo, Dioscorus (one of the Tall Brothers), and "Isidore the Confessor."[33] *Lausiac History* 10 also connects Melania with Pambo, the teacher of the Tall Brothers. The Coptic *Life of Pambo* even gives her the honor of placing her in Pambo's cell when he dies (par. 6); like Antony passing on his clothing to Athanasius and Serapion in the *Life of Antony*, Pambo gives Melania a basket he has woven so she will remember him, a memento she keeps until her death. The Coptic *Life of Macarius of Alexandria* 2 glorifies Melania even more: there she is called "queen of the Romans" and, explicitly like Athanasius now, receives a sheepskin from Macarius just before his death. From Nitria, the Coptic *Life of Pambo* reports (par. 5), Melania "went into the great desert of Scetis and built a church for Abba Isidore the priest."[34] This desert sojourn, however, was to end precipitously.

During Melania and Rufinus' stay in Egypt, the emperor Valens (364–378), an Arian, ordered the persecution of Nicene Christians.[35]

---

[32]Jerome calumnied Melania, *cuius nomen nigredinis testatur perfidiae tenebras* ("whose black name testifies to the darkness of her perfidy"); *Epistle* 133.3 (CSEL 56.246).

[33]*LH* 46.1 (Meyer, 123); Evelyn White, 2.75–76, who dates their visit to 373–374. Epiphanius, who may have instigated the Origenist crisis by attacking Origen in his works, was writing in the mid 370s, the same time that Melania and Rufinus were in Egypt; Guillaumont, *Les "Kephalaia Gnostica,"* 58 n. 42, notes the "striking" agreement between the dates of Melania's visit to "Origenist" monks in Egypt and Epiphanius' attack on Origenism. On Isidore, see Socrates *EH* 6.9. On Melania and Rufinus, see Francis X. Murphy, "Melania the Elder: A Biographical Note," *Traditio* 5 (1947): 59–77 (he opts for their meeting in Alexandria, 67), and *Rufinus of Aquileia (345–411): His Life and Works* (Washington, D.C.: Catholic University of America Press, 1945).

[34]This Isidore is not the same as Isidore of Alexandria, "the Confessor" and enemy of Theophilus.

[35]On this period see Evelyn White, 2.76–80. In 376, Valens revoked the sentences of exile on the Nicenes.

In a striking foreshadowing of the rout of the Origenist monks in 399, because of persecution by the Arian archbishop of Alexandria, Melania fled to Palestine with some Nitrian monks, including Ammonius, Paphnutius, Pambo, and Isidore of Alexandria; by late in the 370s Rufinus had joined Melania in Palestine.[36] Evagrius came to see Melania around 382, and their relationship was obviously a close one: Evagrius wrote his *Ad virginem* (*To a Virgin*) either for Melania or one of her nuns, and his famous—or infamous—*Letter to Melania* was written either to Melania or Rufinus.[37] In this letter Evagrius posits an Origenist fall of minds into bodies and declares that in that fall human beings have lost the image of God, a theological position that will figure prominently in the Anthropomorphite controversy (see below).[38] Palladius later visited Melania, and speaks of her in glowing terms in *Lausiac History* 46, 54, and 55. When Evagrius arrived in Egypt, he came under the care of "Isidore the elder, guestmaster of the church of Alexandria," who had been a monk in the desert.[39] Evagrius thus had direct or indirect associations with numerous pro-Origenist figures, several of whom—Isidore, the Tall Brothers—would suffer banishment as a result of the Anthropomorphite controversy.

Evagrius seems to have been especially close to Ammonius, the most eminent of the Tall Brothers; according to Palladius, the latter was "a very learned scholar," which would make him a natural friend for Evagrius.[40] In *Antirrheticos* 6.16, Evagrius reports a visit that he

[36]*LH* 46.3; Paulinus of Nola *Epistle* 29.11; Rufinus *EH* 2.2–4; Socrates *EH* 4.24; Sozomen *EH* 6.20, Cassian *Conference* 18.7.

[37]On the *Ad virginem*, see Suzanna Elm, "Evagrius Ponticus' *Sententiae ad Virginem*," *Dumbarton Oaks Papers* 45 (1991) 97–120. On the letter, see "Letter to Melania," trans. Martin Parmentier, "Evagrius of Pontus' 'Letter to Melania,'" *Bijdragen, tijdschrift voor filosofie en theologie*, 46 (1985): 2–38.

[38]On this theological theme, see Appendix IV.

[39]*LH* 1; Palladius says he even saw his cell in Nitria. Sozomen, *EH* 8.2, confirms Isidore's position, but says he was a monk in Scetis. Palladius curiously notes that Isidore died a "peaceful death" fifteen years later and says nothing about his fall from Theophilus' good graces.

[40]*LH* 11.1 (Meyer, 46).

and Ammonius made to John of Lycopolis in the Thebaid, probably the same visit recounted in *Lausiac History* 35 (where Ammonius' presence has been excised), made shortly before John's death either at the end of 394 or the beginning of 395.[41] According to Palladius (*LH* 24.1), Evagrius and Ammonius were at the center of the Origenist group at Kellia.[42]

Even more intriguing are Evagrius' connections with two other great monastic figures who apparently escaped censorship or censure in later anti-Origenist inquisitions: Macarius of Egypt (the Great) and Macarius of Alexandria.[43] Evagrius begins par. 93 of his *Praktikos* with "The vessel of election, the elder Macarius the Egyptian, asked me . . ." which shows that Evagrius knew Macarius. (The condensed version of this saying that passed into the *Apophthegmata* excises Evagrius).[44] Numerous apophthegms of the Coptic *Virtues of Macarius* are accounts of conversations, "not without some verisimilitude," between Evagrius and Macarius.[45] In the Coptic *Life of Macarius* 2, in a sentence not found in the *Lausiac History*, the narrator says that "Abba Evagrius was also very close" to Macarius the Great, and that "he himself told me about a few of his virtues too."[46]

[41]See Butler, 1.181–82.

[42]*Hoi peri ton hagion Ammonion kai Euagrion suntichontes.*

[43]On this subject, see especially Guillaumont, "Le problème des deux Macaires," and Gabriel Bunge, "Évagre le Pontique et les deux Macaires."

[44]Evagrius Ponticus, *The Praktikos [and] Chapters on Prayer*, trans. John Eudes Bamberger (Kalamazoo: Cistercian, 1981), 39. *Praktikos* 91 and 95 also passed into the *Systematic Apophthegmata* with Evagrius' name conspicuously absent; see Jean-Claude Guy, ed., *Les Apophtegmes des Pères: Collection systématique. Chapitres I–IX* (SC 387; Paris: Cerf, 1993), 103–104. Since Macarius the Great was at Scetis, one might suppose that this passage refers to Macarius the Alexandrian, but the condensed version is found under *apophthegmata* credited to Macarius the Great, and this attribution is supported by Guillaumont, "Le problème," 49–50. Since condensation is common in the *Apophthegmata*, the excision of Evagrius does not necessarily demonstrate censorship, though that remains a possibility.

[45]Guillaumont, "Le problème," 57. For the *Virtues*, see 17, 39, 42, 76, 77, 81; Am 137–38, 157–58, 160–61, 195–96, and 200–202.

[46]This may also suggest discipleship on Evagrius' part (*nafkeh erof*; Crum 133a). BV translate as "Évagre . . . était très lié avec lui," and Chaîne "Évagrius . . . qui était son grand émule."

Given that Evagrius settled for good at the Cells (Kellia), his relationship with Macarius of Alexandria, who was a priest at Kellia, was probably even closer: in *Praktikos* 94 Evagrius reports that he "went over to see the holy Father Macarius [of Alexandria] at the very hottest time of day."[47] The chapter on Macarius of Alexandria in the *Lausiac History* (18) is by far the longest chapter in the book (the chapter on Macarius of Egypt is the second longest). As Antoine Guillaumont, one of the foremost scholars on Evagrius, has concluded, "The relationship between this Macarius and Evagrius seems to have been very close, Macarius being in sympathy with the group of Origenist monks of which Evagrius was the most conspicuous."[48]

Thus, the Anthropomorphite clash owed something, perhaps a great deal, to "the personal associations of its contestants."[49] Evagrius seems to have been the hub of these associations; indeed, the spiritual make-up of monasticism at Kellia may well have been more "Evagrian" than the *Apophthegmata* would lead us to believe.[50] One can not merely dismiss the persons associated with Evagrius as minor figures huddled around a heretic; the Macarii, two of the most eminent figures of the ancient—and modern Coptic—Church are involved. Furthermore (to take the other side for a moment), Palladius makes it abundantly clear that these personal associations were cemented together by (had their origins in?) an abiding respect for Origen, another "heretic": both Ammonius and Melania had memorized hundreds of thousands of lines of "the highly reputable

[47]Evagrius, *Praktikos* 94 (Bamberger, 40). On the identification here as the Alexandrian, see Guillaumont, "Le problème," 52, and Bunge, "Evagre le Pontique et les deux Macaires," 221 and 223.

[48]Guillaumont, "Le problème," 52. For a list of occasions where Evagrius mentions the two Macarii in his works, see Bunge, "Évagre le Pontique et les deux Macaires," 219; Bunge has also studied, 325–328, the similarities between the ascetics of Evagrius and Macarius of Alexandria.

[49]Clark, *The Origenist Controversy*, 44. Mark Sheridan, "The Modern Historiography of Early Egyptian Monasticism," *Studia Anselmiana* (forthcoming), has criticized some of Clark's conclusions: "There is no doubt that Evagrius' writings figured in the condemnations of the sixth century, but that does not justify the assumption that they were at the center of the dispute 150 years earlier."

[50]Bunge, "Évagre le Pontique et les deux Macaires," 356.

writings of Origen."[51] For the Church historian Socrates, the Anthropomorphite monks, unlike the Origenists, were "simple ascetics" unlettered in the higher realms of "philosophic" (that is, monastic) thought, and Theophilus, endowed with a "hasty and malignant temperment," was greedy and acquisitive. For Cassian, the Anthropomorphites were "rather simple"; possessed of an "errant naiveté," they were "ensnared" in error.[52] What was this "error"?

Spiritual and Theological (and Political) Aspects of the Anthropomorphite Controversy

According to Socrates (despite his politicizing tendencies), the question was theological in origin: Does God have corporeal existence and human form, or is God incorporeal, without human or any other bodily form? The Anthropomorphites, following descriptions of God in Scripture and the affirmation that human beings are made in God's image and likeness, believed that God did in fact have anthropomorphite, human, form and characteristics. Those opposed to them, following Platonic—and Origenist—thought, believed that God was incorporeal. Archbishop Theophilus agreed with those opposed to Anthropomorphism and in his Paschal or Festal Letter of 399 (no longer extant) apparently condemned Anthropomorphism. Later, however, when confronted by angry Anthropomorphite monks, Theophilus reversed himself and condemned the Origenists. For Palladius and Socrates, Theophilus' motives were entirely political and expedient: he desired to save his ecclesiastical hide and at the same time sought revenge against the Origenist Tall Brothers because they had sniffed out (Palladius and Socrates say) the bishop's cupidity; Palladius even charges that Theophilus bribed a young man to accuse Isidore of Alexandria of sodomy.[53] Theophilus had once

[51]The opinion is Palladius', *LH* 11.4 (Meyer, 47); see also 55.3.

[52]For English translations, see Socrates *EH* 142–143 and Ramsey, 371–372.

[53]Palladius *Dialogue* 6 (Coleman-Norton, 22–23); see Clark, *The Origenist Controversy*, 105–120.

supported Isidore for the see of Constantinople (against John Chrysostom), but turned against him and excommunicated him. According to the Church historian Sozomen, Isidore returned to the desert and joined the Tall Brothers, who interceded on his behalf.[54] Theophilus imprisoned one of the monks, but the others joined him, forcing the bishop to free them. This, says Sozomen, was Theophilus' prime motivation for his hatred of the Origenist monks.[55] Theophilus routed the Origenist monks in 399; Palladius says that Isidore and the Tall Brothers, along with priests and deacons and some three hundred other monks, fled to Palestine, then to Constantinople.[56]

Most scholars have concurred in this political/ecclesiastical assessment of a vengeful, vindictive, raging Theophilus.[57] No doubt Church politics played a part (they always do), but recent research has suggested that there was much more of a theological undercurrent to the controversy. Socrates himself hints at this. When the Anthropomorphite monks confront Theophilus and demand a retraction, they interestingly make a single demand: "anathematize Origen's book; for some drawing arguments from them oppose themselves to our opinion." Theophilus says that he himself disapproves of Origen's works. Socrates reports that Theophilus had had theological discussions about the incorporeality of God with the Tall Brothers who argued that God having human form "would involve the necessary accompaniment of the passions." This argument had been "demonstrated by the ancient writers and especially Origen."[58]

[54]Sozomen *EH* 8.12; Clark, *The Origenist Controversy*, 47.

[55]Evelyn White, 2.135–137.

[56]Palladius *Dialogue* 7 (Coleman-Norton, 39); Sozomen *EH* 8.13; Socrates *EH* 6.9. Bunge, "Évagre le Pontique et les deux Macaires," 356, believes that Origenists comprised almost all the monks of Kellia. Guillaumont, *Les "Kephalaia Gnostika,"* 59, suggests that on the whole the number of Origenist monks was "quite restricted" while the Anthropomorphites made up the majority.

[57]See Evelyn White, 135, and J. N. D. Kelly, *Golden Mouth: The Story of John Chrysostom* (Ithaca: Cornell UP, 1995), 192, although Evelyn White argues, 86, that Evagrius was the "intellectual center" of the Origenists and that his teaching was regarded by some as suspect. For Theophilus' side of things, see Clark, *The Origenist Controversy*, 105–120.

[58]Socrates *EH* 6.7.

The passions, and their abatement and even extirpation, were perhaps the chief concern of Evagrius. And Evagrius was known to be both a follower of Origen and closely associated with Ammonius, the leader of the Tall Brothers.[59] It seems that Evagrius was the "unindicted co-conspirator" of the Origenists, their theological and spiritual leader whose thought undergirded their opposition to the Anthropomorphites.

Although Evagrius is missing from the ancient accounts of the Anthropomorphite-Origenist controversy, his theology, "more origenistic than Origen himself," may have been central to the conflict.[60] Evagrius' starting point was the incorporeality, simplicity, and imagelessness of God. This is not mere Platonism. Trinitarian thinking lies behind Evagrius' "iconoclasm." In the Coptic *Life of Evagrius* (drastically condensed in Greek), three demons visit Evagrius, disguised as "servants of the Church":

> The first said to him, "I am a Eunomian. I have come to you so you might tell me whether the Father is begotten or unbegotten." Apa Evagrius said to him, "I will not answer you because you have asked a bad question, for it is not right to talk about the nature of the Unbegotten and to inquire whether it is begotten or unbegotten" (par. 29).

Evagrius ruled out all attributes of God (quality, quantity, begotten, unbegotten), even biblical ones, so it follows that he rejected the

---

[59] See *LH* 24.2 for "Saints Ammonius and Evagrius." For more on the Tall Brothers, see Evelyn White, 130–131, and for the later intertwining of their lives with that of John Chrysostom, Kelly, *Golden Mouth*, 191–202.

[60] Clark, *The Origenist Controversy*, 43–84; she acknowledges, 44, that Antoine and Claire Guillaumont preceded her. Sheridan, "Modern Historiography," demurs: "the original causes were not predominantly certain personalities, Epiphanius and Theophilus in particular, as Tillemont perceived." The quotation belongs to Hans Urs von Balthasar, *Metaphysik und Mystik*, 42, cited by Murphy, 254, and Guillaumont, *Les "Kephalaia Gnostika*," 32 (see his further comments on 32 n. 76). For a review of scholarly opinions on Evagrius' Origenism, see Guillaumont, 40–42 and, for an outstanding summary of Evagrius' Origenist thought vis-à-vis his opponents, Guillaumont, 102–123.

Anthropomorphite belief that God has human attributes.[61] Evagrius was "radically anti-imagistic."[62] For Evagrius, images arouse
emotions and impede *apatheia*, the passionless peace required for
contemplation of, and ultimate union with, God. The mind should
be completely free of images so that God can illuminate the person
praying.

Evagrius was especially anti-imagistic in his teaching on prayer;
in fact, Evagrius' teaching may have started the Anthropomorphite
controversy.[63] It is important to understand here that this controversy was not waged in academic journals or conferences but was
entered into, felt, by monks whose chief occupation in life was prayer;
thus, the controversy was not abstract theological speculation but
intimately affected the monks' life of prayer. For Evagrius, the goal of
such a life was to get beyond images, but the majority of monks did
not share this goal. John Cassian's story of Serapion, recounted
above, clearly illustrates this; in modern terms, it shows the connection between orthopraxis, right practice, and orthodoxy, right belief.
Cassian, despite his previous condescension toward the Athropo-
morphites, quietly, almost guiltily, acknowledges that he and his
companions were "greatly shaken" by Serapion's *cri de coeur*: "They
have taken my God from me, and I have no one to lay hold of, nor do
I know whom I should adore or address."[64] Clearly, if Serapion's heart
was "cleansed" of images, it was left broken; iconoclasm ceases to be
theoretical here and has profoundly personal consequences.

This account of Serapion's "conversion" takes place in the midst
of a Conference by Abba Isaac devoted to "pure"—that is, imageless—prayer.[65] Is Isaac a stand-in for Evagrius?[66] Cassian naturally

---

[61]Guillaumont, Les *"Kephalaia Gnostica,"* 50, shows the similarities between
Kephalaia Gnostica 5.51 and *Theological Discourse* 2.3 of Gregory of Nazianzus, thus
pointing once again to Cappadocia.

[62]Clark, *The Origenist Controversy*, 63; see also 61–62.

[63]Guillaumont, Les *"Kephalaia Gnostica,"* 61.

[64]*Conference* 10.3.4–5; Ramsey, 373.

[65]See *Virtues of Saint Macarius* 41 in *Saint Macarius the Spiritbearer* where
Macarius says, "Concentrate on this name of our Lord Jesus Christ with a contrite

(as a follower of Evagrius) thought that Serapion had been "led on by some new delusion of the demons," but Isaac assures him that it was ignorance that caused the old man's plight—"the ignorance that characterized the earliest pagans":

> For, as is the way of that error, according to which they used to worship demons in human form, now they also hold that the incomprehensible and ineffable majesty of the true Deity should be adored under the limitations of some image, and they do not believe that anything can be grasped and understood if no image of it is set up, which they can always approach with their petitions, circumscribe in their minds, and keep constantly before their eyes.[67]

Against such "superstition" Isaac (Cassian, Evagrius) places pure prayer: to the extent that the mind

> withdraws from the contemplation of earthly and material things, its state of purity lets it progress and causes Jesus to be seen by the soul's inward gaze. . . . But they alone see his Godhead with purest eyes who, mounting from humble and earthly tasks and thoughts, go off with him to the lofty mountain of the desert which, free from the uproar of every earthly thought and disturbance, removed from every taint of vice, and exalted with the purest faith and with soaring virtue, reveals the glory of his face and the image of his brightness to those who deserve to look upon him with the clean gaze of the soul.[68]

heart, the words welling up from your lips and drawing you to them. And do not depict him with an image in your mind but concentrate on calling to him: 'Our Lord Jesus, have mercy on me.'"

[66]Bunge, "Évagre le Pontique et les deux Macaires," 342: "It is equally well known that this famous Abba Isaac speaks the language of Evagrius."

[67]*Conference* 10.6.1–2 (Ramsey, 374–375).

[68]*Conference* 10.5.1 (Ramsey, 373–374).

The goal of such contemplation for the solitary was union with God, when "one's whole way of life and all the yearnings of one's heart become a single and continuous prayer," which Cassian describes in one of the most beautiful passages in patristic literature (Abba Isaac is speaking):

> This will be the case when every love, every desire, every effort, every undertaking, every thought of ours, everything that we live, that we speak, that we breathe, will be God, and when that unity which the Father now has with the Son and which the Son has with the Father will be carried over into our understanding and our mind, so that, just as he loves us with a sincere and pure and indissoluble love, we too may be joined to him with a perpetual and inseparable love and so united with him that whatever we breathe, whatever we understand, whatever we speak, may be God.[69]

Given this goal, and the imageless means of attaining it, it is hardly surprising that images were anathema to Evagrius.[70] What may be more surprising is that Evagrius' iconoclastic theology and spirituality presumed a more pessimistic anthropology than did the Anthropomorphites.[71] The latter, following the account in Genesis, believed that humans are made in the image and likeness of God and retain some form of that image, even after the fall. As a result, humans can form an image of God in their mind. The monk Aphou,

[69] *Conference* 10.7.2 (Ramsey, 375–76).

[70] For a good discussion of the tension in Evagrius' thought concerning images, see Columba Stewart, "Imageless Prayer and the Theological Vision of Evagrius Ponticus," *Journal of Early Christian Studies* 9.2 (2001): 173–204.

[71] See Michael O'Laughlin, "The Anthropology of Evagrius Ponticus and its Sources," in C. Kannengiesser and W. Petersen, eds., *Origen of Alexandria: His World and His Legacy* (Notre Dame: Univ. of Notre Dame Press, 1988), 357–73. For the more positive, though Origenist, anthropology of Didymus the Blind, see Placid Solari, "Christ as Virtue in Didymus the Blind," in Harriet A. Luckman and Linda Kulzer, eds., *Purity of Heart in Early Ascetic and Monastic Literature* (Collegeville: Liturgical Press, 1999), 67–88.

in his discussion with Archbishop Theophilus, presents their side of things: "in exalting the glory of God in [Theophilus' festal letter of 399], it emphasized human weakness, and the person who had dictated it said 'this weakness is not the image of God,' understanding 'this weakness' to be we who bear the image, that is, we human beings" ([5]; see Appendix IV for Aphou's statement).

Georges Florovsky summarizes the theological and anthropological issue at stake in Aphou's statement:

> The sting of his argument was directed against the denial of God's image *in man*, and there was no word whatever about any "human form" *in God*. Aphou only contended that man, even in his present condition and in spite of all his misery and destitution, had to be regarded still as being created in the image of God, and must be, for that reason, respected. Aphou was primarily concerned with man's dignity and honor. Theophilus, on the other hand, was embarrassed by man's misery and depravity.[72]

For Evagrius, following Origen, human beings had lost the image of God (a belief that Theophilus apparently originally held; see Appendix IV); therefore, all that remains for us are (false) images—thoughts, dreams, fantasies—that distract us from God.[73] Images imply bodies, and Evagrius followed Origen in teaching that bodies are a secondary addition to the pure, incorporeal "naked *nous*" created at creation. At the end, bodies will be discarded (destroyed, not transformed), and the *nous* will return to God.[74] For the Evagrians,

[72]Georges Florovsky, "Theophilus of Alexandria and Apa Aphou of Pemdje," in *Harry Austryn Wolfson Jubilee Volume* (Jerusalem: American Academy for Jewish Research 1965), 275–310, repr. in Georges Florovsky, *Collected Works*, vol. 4, *Aspects of Church History* (Belmont, MA: Nordland, 1975), 97–129, at 119. Gould, "The Image of God," also suggests, 550–552, that the question of whether or not human beings retain the image of God was more central to the conflict.

[73]See Clark, *The Origenist Controversy*, 75.

[74]Evagrius *Kephalaia gnostica* 2.77, 3.66, 6.20, 6.85; Guillaumont, *Les "Kephalaia Gnostica*," 109. Evagrius *Epistula ad Melaniam* 5–6 (Parmentier, 11–13).

the way to God was paved with broken images.[75] The Anthropomorphite controversy was, ultimately, for *both* those who followed
Evagrius *and* for the Anthropomorphites soteriological. Soteriological concerns, however, have a way of shaping the way the history,
tradition, and texts of the Church come down to us. Such is the case
with the *Lausiac History* of Palladius.

The Lausiac History and the Coptic Palladiana[76]

"The outcome of the Origenist controversy in Egypt clearly
impacted the literary record of asceticism. The received tradition became an anti-Origenist tradition."[77]

In chapter 38.11 of the *Lausiac History* Evagrius debates three
"demons disguised as clergy": a Eunomian, an Arian, and an Apollinarian.[78] The debate does not last long: Palladius supposedly (the
use of this adverb will be clear in a minute) devotes only a few lines
to the contest and Evagrius defeats the faux clerics "with his knowledge and a few words." This version, however, does not seem to be
the one that Palladius originally wrote: the original was much
longer. The Coptic *Life of Evagrius*, although fragmentary (it ends
with this encounter, whose conclusion is missing), preserves a much

[75]Rowan Williams, *The Wound of Knowledge* (Cambridge, MA: Cowley, 1991), 70,
has critiqued Evagrius' theology as "one charged with a systemic *suspicion* of images
and concepts of God, the world and self. Evagrius' may be an 'imageless' prayer; but
we need Gregory [of Nyssa]'s scepticism to prevent imageless prayer itself from
becoming an idol, a stopping point." Stewart, "Imageless Prayer," 195, believes that
Evagrius "found in the sacred texts of Christianity metaphors that could suggest [his
own deepest experience] without trapping it within the limits he considered fatal to
'true prayer.'"

[76]Portions of this section are paraphrased from BV with appropriate citation.

[77]James E. Goehring, *Ascetics, Society, and the Desert: Studies in Early Egyptian
Monasticism* (Studies in Antiquity and Christianity; Harrisburg, PA: Trinity, 1999),
208.

[78]Such a debate may be modelled on Antony's contest with pagan philosophers
in *Life of Antony* 72–80.

longer account of Evagrius' debate with the theologically-minded demons (par. 29). The Greek of the *Lausiac History*, by contrast, is obviously an epitome of the confrontation, one of three stories grouped together under the heading of "demons or spirits that bothered Evagrius."[79]

At first one might suspect the longer Coptic version of being an expansion of a short Greek text, but this is highly unlikely, for several reasons. First, by chance a Greek version of this story has survived, one that is very close to the Coptic version and which the Coptic has clearly translated.[80] The Greek text leaves us with two choices: either Palladius wrote a long version of the story and later considerably shortened it and "regrouped" it, or he wrote a long version and a later editor did the curtailing. Second, the long version is theologically accurate. The Arian denies the divinity of the Holy Spirit; this is not a classic Arian position, but precisely captures the point of view of the Homoians, whom Nicenes such as Athanasius branded as "Arian."[81] The Eunomian's concerns about whether the Father is begotten or unbegotten are equally accurate: the Eunomians argued that only the Father, strictly speaking, was *agennētos*, unbegotten. The Apollinarian position, that Christ's human intellect was replaced by divinity, is also accurate. Finally, Evagrius' assertion,

[79]The Coptic *Life* preserves the first two stories separately (pars. 22 and 23), at some remove from the third (par. 29). The structure of the Greek epitome is more evident in Greek than in the English (Meyer) or Italian (Barchiesi) translations I consulted: [1] *Toutōi ōchlēsen* . . . [2] *Allote palin ōchlēsen* . . . [3] *Toutōi treis . . . daimones.* Neither English nor Italian duplicates the initial *toutōi* at the beginning of [1] and [3], but the Italian (Bartelink, 201) better preserves the repetition of *ōchlēsen* in [1] and [2] with "tormentò" and "tormentarlo" than English "bothered" and "tormented" (Meyer, 113–114).

[80]The Greek text was published by J.-B. Cotelerius (Cotelier), in *Ecclesiae graecae monumenta* III (Paris, 1686), 117–20 and reproduced from Paris Gk 1220 f. 271v by Butler, 1.132–35. A French translation may be found in BV 173–175. For an English translation, see Appendix III below. Part II of the text, the confrontation with the Arian, is considerably longer in Greek than in Coptic; parts I, the Eunomian, and Part III, the Apollinarian, correspond closely in Greek and Coptic, although the end of Part III is missing in Coptic.

[81]See R. P. C. Hanson, *The Search for the Christian Doctrine of God* (Edinburgh: T & T Clark, 1988), 557ff.; for their views on the Spirit, see 740ff.

against the Apollinarian, of the fully human mind of Christ is more Greek than Coptic and is not likely to have emanated from post-Chalcedonian Egypt.[82]

Even more importantly, Evagrius' own writings corroborate the substance and details of the long version.[83] When the first demon, the Eunomian, asks Evagrius "whether the Father is begotten or unbegotten," Evagrius replies, "I will not answer you because you have asked a bad question, for it is not right to talk about the nature of the Unbegotten and to inquire whether it is begotten or unbegotten." In *Gnostikos* 27 Evagrius makes the same argument: "Do not speak about God inconsiderately and never define the Divinity. For definitions belong to created and composite beings."[84] Eunomian theology sought to define the essence of God as "ingenerateness," and since the Son was "generated" by the Father, then the Son could not be God. But Evagrius refutes this hyper-rationalism. In *Kephalaia Gnostika* 5.51 he attacks the Eunomians directly and in *Gnostikos* 41 declares: "Every proposition has as a predicate either a genus or a distinction or a species or a property or an accident or that which is composed of these—but in regard to the Trinity, none [of this terminology] that has just been said is admissible. Let the ineffable be adored in silence!"[85] It is reasonable to conclude, therefore, that Palladiuis, who knew Evagrius, wrote the longer—accurate—version of *Lausiac History* 38.11, found in the Coptic *Life of Evagrius*, which confronts us with a better, fuller text than the one found in the *Lausiac*

[82]For Evagrius' Trinitarian views, see his *Epistula fidei*, long attributed to Saint Basil (as Epistle VIII) but now recognized as belonging to Evagrius; *Saint Basil: The Letters*, trans. Roy J. Deferrari (Cambridge: Harvard UP, 1950), 46–92.

[83]I wish to thank William Harmless, S.J. for alerting me to these passages and for giving me his translation of the *Gnostikos*.

[84]Antoine Guillaumont, ed., *Évagre le Pontique: Le Gnostique ou a celui qui est devenu digne de la science* (Sources chrétiennes 356; Paris: Cerf, 1989), 132–33; Harmless trans.

[85]Guillaumont, ed., 166–67; Harmless, trans. See Gendle, "Cappadocian Elements," 374–378. See Socrates *EH* 3.7. The five technical terms (genus, distinction, species, property, accident) that Evagrius cites here are from ancient logic; Porphyry's *Eisagoge* attributes them to Aristotle's *Categories*. See Michael O'Laughlin, "Origenism in the Desert" (Th.D. Thesis, Harvard University, 1987), 196.

History itself.[86] This leads directly to the question of the other Coptic *Lives* that represent longer versions than those preserved in Greek.

Palladius wrote the *Lausiac History* around 420 when he was a bishop, about thirty years after his sojourn in Egypt. What were his sources? More than one monk of whom Palladius speaks was dead before Palladius came to Egypt and he distinguishes between those whom he saw or learned from and those whom he learned about from others. Did he get other sources from Evagrius, his spiritual master? From primitive collections of the *Apophthegmata*? Evagrius concludes his *Praktikos* (91–100) with a small collection of "excellent sayings and deeds" of earlier monks, most notably Macarius the Great.[87] A passage in the Coptic *Life of Macarius of Alexandria* 1, the story of the visit of Macarius of Alexandria to the garden of Jannes and Jambres, comes from Evagrius, *Antirrhetikos* 4.23, and thus shows the literary dependence of the Coptic *Life* on Evagrius, or an Evagrian tradition.[88]

The four Coptic *Lives*—Pambo, Evagrius, Macarius of Egypt, Macarius of Alexandria—are principally contained in Coptic synaxaries where they were preserved for liturgical reading, but without a doubt were originally written in Greek.[89] What is the relationship between the *Lausiac History* and these Coptic fragments? It is obvious right off that the latter are not mere translations of the former. One possibility is that there were two recensions of the *Lausiac History*, one short and one long, attested by fragments in Greek, Syriac, Latin, and Coptic. The suggestion of two recensions, though

[86]The only other possibility is that a later (Greek) writer, with access to Evagrius' works, wrote the long version. Even if that is the case, the long version must belong to the fourth-fifth century.

[87]Evagrius *Praktikos* (Bamberger, 39–41).

[88]BV 36–37. Guillaumont, "Le problème," 52, points out that Evagrius, Palladius, and the Latin version of the *Historia Monachorum* attribute the story to this Macarius, and not to Macarius the Great as does the Greek *Historia Monachorum*.

[89]BV 18. Since the Mss. are in Bohairic, they are relatively late (10th c.), but undoubtedly rely on earlier Mss. See Mark Sheridan, "Histoire Lausiaque 1141" (Review of BV), *Collectanea Cisterciensia* 57.3 (1995): 548–552.

attractive, has too many problems associated with it. It is better to see these four *Lives* as, in Gabriel Bunge's words, a "lateral tradition," one with a distinctly Palladian character. This tradition is very well informed about details concerning Scetis; there is no indication that *Lausiac History* 72 and 73 (preserved in Syriac; see Appendix II) or the long recension of the *Life of Evagrius* were ever part of the *Lausiac History*.[90] Therefore, one must make a clear distinction between "Lausiac" and "Palladian": the former designates material pertaining to the *Lausiac History*, while the latter refers to writings that have Palladius as their author.

Certain indications within and outside the *Lausiac History* lead to the conclusion that the Palladian material distributed throughout the Coptic synaxaries, but also attested elsewhere, belongs to another, earlier, work by Palladius. The parts that remain indicate that it was dedicated (exclusively?) to a history of Egyptian anchoritic monasticism in the fourth century. Socrates (*EH* 4.23) speaks of a "treatise" by "the *monk* Palladius, who was a disciple of Evagrius" (emphasis added) and relates three stories about Abba Pambo that are found in the Coptic *Life* but not in the *Lausiac History*.[91] It is reasonable to suggest that Socrates is referring to a work that Palladius wrote when he was a monk in Egypt, long before he became a bishop (Socrates is aware elsewhere in his *History* that Palladius did become a bishop). We know little about this treatise except that it concerned the "deeds and experiences and discourses" of monks, both male and female. Besides deeds (*facta*) there were also "the things they said for the benefit of those who heard them [*verba*]"[92] In addition, Socrates makes the odd remark that "both Evagrius and Palladius flourished a short time after the death of Valens," that is, after 378. Such a statement makes sense if Socrates

[90]BV 78.

[91]Socrates *EH* 4.23. Pars. 2, (5, 10), and 12 (the last = *AP* Pambo 4).

[92]BV 78–79. Antoine Guillaumont has drawn attention to the importance of both word *and* deed among the early desert monks; see "L'Enseignement spirituel des moines d'Égypte," repr. in his *Études sur la spiritualité de l'orient chrétien* (Bégrolles-en-Mauges: Bellefontaine, 1996), 81–92.

had before him an early work of Palladius and was thinking of Palladius' discipleship in the desert in the 380s and 390s and not of his later career as bishop, author of the *Lausiac History*, and champion of John Chrysostom.

The *Lausiac History* was destined for a high official, Lausus, in the court of Theodosius II and also for a wider audience; thus it was not limited solely to an Egyptian milieu but embraced equally the eastern world with Syria and Mesopotamia as well as the west with Rome and Campania. The whole was conceived as a kind of autobiography in the form of a history of monasticism in the fourth century.[93] A number of persons who appear in the *Lausiac History*, as shown above, were associated with Origenism, either directly or indirectly: Evagrius, Macarius of Egypt, Macarius of Alexandria, the Tall Brothers, Pambo. The condemnation of Origen in 553 and the subsequent loss of many of his writings was also fatal for Didymus the Blind and Evagrius, virtually all of whose works disappeared in Greek. Around 553 began the systematic suppression of all traces of Origenism in the work of Palladius (see Appendix I, "Seven Goals of Anti-Origenism").[94] Apparently the *Historia Monachorum* also suffered from similar "clumsy and incompetent" anti-Origenistic revising; if that was the case, then it becomes easier to accept parallel expurgating in the *Lausiac History*.[95]

A century ago Dom Cuthbert Butler recognized that there were problems in the text of the *Lausiac History*, that certain "heretical or suspected names that occur throughout the book" had been eliminated and that the text he preferred (G) showed unmistakable anti-Origenist tendencies. The result of this tendency was to eliminate all

[93]BV 79.

[94]BV 24–25. On Evagrius' link with Origenism in the sixth century, see Daley, "What did 'Origenism' Mean?" On the dating, see Gabriel Bunge, "Palladiana," *Studia Monastica*, 32 (1990), esp. 81–84 and 99–102. C. P. Bammel, "Problems of the *Historia Monachorum*," *Journal of Theological Studies*, N.S. 47.1 (1996): 92–104, at 101, suggests that "the possibility of an earlier date should also be considered," but does not say why.

[95]See Bammel, "Problems of the *Historia Monachorum*," 99–101; the characterization is hers, 99. See her list of anti-Origenist "corrections" on 100.

trace of these "heretics"; in the words of René Draguet, a veritable *damnatio memoriae*.[96] Thus the Coptic fragments of Palladius' theorized youthful "History of Egyptian Monasticism" assume great importance. The scholarly debate over these Coptic *Lives* has not been resolved.[97] It is not absolutely certain that Palladius did write an earlier version of the *Lausiac History*. The existence of the Coptic *Lives*, however, forces us to look at the *Lausiac History* anew, and especially to take a fresh look at questions regarding its editing and transmission in antiquity and the almost certain censorship regarding Evagrius and other Origenists.

There is now just too much evidence to accept the received text of the *Lausiac History* without question. The account of the follower of Hieracas, Evagrius' debate with the three theological demons, the much longer Coptic version of the *Life of Evagrius*, chapters [72] and [73] of the Syriac *Lausiac History*, and the numerous differences between the Greek and Coptic versions of Palladius' work force a reconsideration: either (1) Palladius wrote two versions of the *Lausiac History*; (2) he wrote an earlier, "Egyptian," version; or (3) the *Lausiac History* was heavily edited after his death and the Coptic has managed to preserve some earlier, unexpurgated readings.[98] The second and third possibilities, together, seem most likely. Whatever is finally decided about the origins of these four *Lives*, those who care about early Egyptian monasticism will be grateful for the precious information that these Coptic fragments have preserved for us.[99] The historical, theological, and spiritual themes that they present still give us much to reflect on and consider.

[96] BV 20.

[97] See Sheridan, "Histoire Lausiaque," 548–552.

[98] For suggestions on the numerous versions of the *Historia Monachorum*, see Bammel, "Problems of the *Historia Monachorum*," 101.

[99] BV 79.

CHAPTER ONE

The Life of Pambo

INTRODUCTION

Pambo of Nitria

Pambo, perhaps influenced by Saint Antony the Great, probably came to Nitria not long after Amoun, who had founded monasticism there about 315. Amoun is closely associated with Pior, Or, and Pambo, all of whom figure in the *Lausiac History*.[1] The *Apophthegmata* also show some knowledge of a connection between Amoun and Pambo.[2] Pambo (Pamō in Coptic) was the master of the Tall Brothers and, thus, was connected to Origenism, a detail carefully erased by the anti-Origenist suppression in one manuscript tradition (G) of the *Lausiac History*. He died in 373–74 at the age of 70 and therefore was born at the beginning of the fourth century. One of Pambo's characteristics seems to have been silence: paragraph 2 of the Coptic *Life* (not preserved in Greek but reported by Socrates in his *Ecclesiastical History*) relates how Pambo kept silence for years until he mastered his tongue. A saying in the *Apophthegmata* confirms this characteristic: when Archbishop Theophilus comes to see him and he is asked to speak, Pambo tartly replies, "If he is not edified by my silence, he will not be edified by my speech."[3]

[1] *LH* 8–10; for a full discussion, see Evelyn White, 2.45–54.
[2] *AP* Antony 6, Poemen 75.
[3] *AP* Theophilus 2. As Evelyn White observes, 2.53 n. 12, the attribution to Theophilus is probably incorrect: Pambo died in 373–74 and Theophilus became patriarch in 385.

Pambo seems to have been ordained a priest before 340 and was given the grace of healing.[4] He emphasized monastic poverty and charity: with regard to the former, he said that monks must work for their bread and clothing and that a monk's clothing should be such that he could throw it out of his cell and no one would steal it for three days.[5] With regard to the latter, he apparently instituted a system of giving by the monks.[6] He was well known for his humility and was so humble that no one could look at him because of the glory that shone from him.[7] Antony said that the spirit of God dwelled in Pambo.[8] Abba Poemen saw three special virtues in Pambo: fasting, silence, and great manual labor.[9]

The Coptic Life of Pambo

The most striking thing about the Coptic text of the *Life of Pambo* is what at first seems like a haphazard anti-Origenism, as though the scribe or editor set out to efface all trace of Pambo's links with suspicious Origenist characters (see the Introduction above) but then grew drowsy or indifferent and forgot about his duties: instead of teaching the four Tall Brothers, Pambo instructs only two of them, and one fellow (who unfortunately shares a name with the heretical Origen) becomes "John" (Par. 3; *LH* 10.1). In the *Lausiac History* this Origen is identified as Pambo's steward, but in the Coptic *Life of Pambo* the steward becomes "Theodore" (pars. 5, 6, 9; *LH* 10.3, 10.6, 10.7); a bit later (in a passage with no parallel in the *Lausiac History*), however, Pambo takes some money and gives it "to his servant named Origen, who is still living and performing the job of steward that the old man gave him" (par. 14).

[4] *AP* Macarius of Egypt 2; Evelyn White, 2.54.
[5] *AP* Pambo 6, pars. 8 and 15 below.
[6] Par. 16 below.
[7] *AP* Pambo 1.
[8] *AP* Poemen 75.
[9] *AP* Poemen 150.

Although conspiracy theories can be attractive and entertaining, there is probably a better explanation for the seeming anti-Origenism of the Coptic *Life of Pambo*. The clue may well lie with the servant Origen: he is not excluded, but displaced.[10] It does not seem plausible that an anti-Origenist editor excluded two of the Tall Brothers and turned the servant into Abba John, and then forgot to exclude the other two brothers and let the servant Origen show up later. If the editor really was anti-Origenist, why not exclude altogether even the names of Dioscorus and Amoun, the other two Tall Brothers, and efface the servant named Origen?

Instead, what if this *Life of Pambo* was an early draft of what was to appear later in the *Lausiac History*, an early work of (as Socrates says) "Palladius the monk"? When Palladius composed the Greek *Lausiac History* some twenty-five years after his sojourn in Egypt, circumstances had decisively changed: there had occurred the bloody battle (both theologically and, apparently, literally) with Theophilus, the exile of the Tall Brothers, and the deposition of John Chrysostom. Twenty-five years after his time in the desert, Palladius was revising things in light of drastically changed circumstances. In the 390s, Palladius the monk may have known only two Tall Brothers, or at least associated only two of them with Pambo. In the 420s, after the four Tall Brothers had become internationally famous, Palladius would associate all four with Pambo, thereby showing how venerable and traditional their monasticism was. In the 390s, Palladius saw Origen as Pambo's faithful servant. In the 420s, he remembered Origen in retrospect not simply as Pambo's faithful servant, but as the "nephew of Dracontius, a marvelous man." In the 420s, Origen has become a "priest" (*LH* 10.6) and a faithful witness to Pambo's death and to the abba's humble habit of saying he really understood very little about Scripture. Origen is also charged with

[10]The name "Origen," however, also suffered excision in manuscripts of the *Historia Monachorum*; see C. P. Bammel, "Problems of the *Historia Monachorum*," 100. "The name," Bammel drily comments, 100, "was regarded with alarm, something which gives an indication of the intellectual level of the reviser who made this excision."

SYNOPTIC TABLE

The Coptic *Life of Pambo & Lausiac History 9–10*

Coptic *Life*	*Lausiac History*
1. Pambo the Righteous	*LH* 9 (Abba Or)
2. Pambo Shows Extraordinary Patience	—
3. Pambo Teaches Others	*LH* 10.1
4. His Hatred of Gold and Silver	*LH* 10.1
5. Melania Talks about Abba Pambo	*LH* 10.2–4
6. The Death of Abba Pambo	*LH* 10.5
7. Abba Isidore Speaks about Abba Pambo	—
8. Abba Pambo's Final Teaching	*LH* 10.6
9. Abba Pambo's Patience in Speaking	*LH* 10.7
10. Abba Pambo Ignores a Large Sum of Money	—
11. Abba Pambo's Good Works and Humility	—
12. Abba Pambo Learns from a Prostitute	—
13. The Faithful Disciple	—
14. Origen the Steward	—
15. We Work for what We Eat and Wear	—
16. Giving to Others	—
17. Abba Pambo Teaches Abba Pihōr a Lesson	*LH* 10.8

the distribution of Melania's donation. It seems that, given the hundreds of monks living in Nitria at the time, Origen had a very significant job; Palladius highlights that role as he retells the story.[11] The material in the Coptic *Life* not found in Greek certainly has the feel of desert ascesis and comports well with what we know of Pambo from the *Lausiac History* and other early sources.

[11]The alternative, as BV suggest regarding the *LH*, is that the anti-Origenist Coptic text was corrupted by "purer" (non-anti-Origenist) texts.

The Dedication and Preface to the *Lausiac History* and the *Life of Pambo* were read together in the Coptic *Synaxary* on the fifth Saturday of Lent.[12]

CONCERNING APA PAMBO
(*LAUSIAC HISTORY* 9–10)[13]

*Pambo the Righteous (*LH 9*)*[14]

1   [92] There appeared in the monastic settlement[15] of Pernouj[16] a certain person named Apa Pambo.[17] *He was second*[18] *after Abba Antony.*[19] *Apa Pambo was thus called alēthinos, "the truthful one,"*[20] concerning whose virtues the whole brotherhood testified. I myself did not meet him in my time there, but the brothers spoke with me about him, saying that that man never said[21] a lie *nor ever commit-*

---

[12]BV 42. The Dedication Letter and Preface are translations of the *LH* without containing supplemental material and thus have been omitted here.

[13]Translated from the text edited by É. Amélineau, *De Historia Lausica, quaenam sit huius ad Monachorum Aegyptiorum historiam scribendam utilitas* (Paris, 1887): 92–104, with corrections by Adalbert de Vogüé, based on Vatican Coptic Codex 64, "Les fragments coptes de l'Histoire Lausiaque: l'édition d'Amélineau et le manuscrit," *Orientalia* 58.3 (1989): 326–32. Numbers in brackets indicate the pagination of Amélineau's text. Gabriel Bunge and Vogüé give a French translation of the corrected text. References to the Greek (Gk) text of the *Lausiac History* are to G. J. M. Bartelink, ed., *Palladio: La Storia Lausiaca* (Milan: Fondazione Lorenzo Valla, 1974), which is a modification of Butler's. Translations of the Gk text are from *Palladius: The Lausiac History*, trans. Robert T. Meyer (Ancient Christian Writers 34; New York: Newman, 1964).

[14]Section titles and paragraphing are my own. Portions in italics are lacking in Gk. Paragraphs without "*LH*" in parentheses lack parallels with the *Lausiac History*. Paragraph numbers do not correspond to *LH* but are given for ease of reference.

[15]Coptic: *pitōou* can mean "mountain" or "monastic settlement," even, in other contexts, "monastery."

[16]That is, Nitria, some 50 kilometers southeast of Alexandria.

[17]His name in Coptic is "Pamō," but since "Pambo" is the customary spelling, I have adopted it here. In the Gk *LH*, this first paragraph refers to Abba Or (*LH* 9).

[18]Reading *mah* with Vogüé rather than Am's *ma*.

[19]In the first few paragraphs the text fluctuates between "Apa" and "Abba."

[20]Gk *alēthinos* means both "truthful" and "faithful."

[21]Reading *mpefje* with Vogüé instead of *ntefje*.

ted a sin with his tongue [Ps 38:2 (LXX)][22] *from the time that he*
became a monk;[23] neither oath nor curse ever came from his mouth,
nor did he ever speak an unnecessary word.[24] *He had a wife and two*
sons, but they themselves did not agree to become monks.

Pambo Shows Extraordinary Patience[25]

2   *When he came to the brothers he went and found an old man and*
said to him, "Teach me a psalm," for he was illiterate, and the old man
began to teach him [93] *this psalm: "I said, 'I will watch my ways so as*
to be unable to sin with my tongue'" [Ps 38:2 (LXX)]. And after the old
man had given him the beginning of the text, Pambo stopped him, say-
ing, "My father, since I haven't yet learned the beginning of the text, I
will not learn the rest." And when Abba Pambo went to his cell, he spent
eight years putting into practice[26] *the saying*[27] *that he had learned, for*
he came into contact with no one, saying, "Unless I first master my
tongue, I will come into contact with no one lest I fall into sin on
account of my tongue." After eight years, he went and paid a visit to the
old man who had given him the psalm. The old man said to him,
"Pambo, why haven't we seen you until today? Why didn't you come to
learn the psalm?" Apa Pambo said to him, "Since I hadn't learned the
first verse, I didn't return to you to get the second since God had not
given me the grace until now to learn it.[28] *In order*[29] *not to act as if I*

[22]See the next par.

[23]See *Life of Antony* 65.1–5 where Antony, in a vision, is judged sinless from the
time he became a monk.

[24]The text up to here parallels *LH* 9, which, however, gives the monk's name as
Or, not Pambo. The sentence referring to Antony is missing in *LH* 9, and in its place
is a reference to Melania (see par. 5 below).

[25]This story is recounted by Socrates *EH* 4.23.

[26]Coptic *eferaskin* = Gk *askein*, "to train oneself through ascetic practice."

[27]Literally "word," *saji*.

[28]Both times in this sentence the text mistakenly has "teach" (*ti sbō, tsabo*) instead
of "learn" (*sbō, sabo*).

[29]Adding *hina* with Vogüé.

despised you, I have come to visit you, my father. For if I learn the first verse, I will come to see you again." [94] *And when he returned to his cell, he stayed there another ten years and did not come into contact with anyone.*

Pambo Teaches Others (LH 10.1)

3   Thus blessed Abba Pambo was in this monastic settlement. It was he who taught Abba Dioscorus the bishop and Abba Amon and Abba John, the nephew of Abba Dracontius the bishop of the town of Hōr.[30]

His Hatred of Gold and Silver (LH 10.1)

4   This Abba Pambo was an admirable person, for his virtues and his accomplishments were great, but he was even more admirable on account of his hatred of gold and silver, as it is written with regard to this subject [Mt 6:19–21].[31]

Melania Talks about Abba Pambo (LH 10.2–4)[32]

5   Blessed Melania[33] talked to me one time about him: "When I first arrived in Alexandria from Rome, Abba Isidore *the priest*[34] told

[30]This list differs in Gk: "He was the teacher of the four brothers, Dioscorus the bishop, Ammonius, Eusebius, and Euthymius, and also of Origen, the nephew of Dracontius, a marvelous man." The first four were the Tall Brothers; see the Introduction to this volume.

[31]The Gk is more compact: "as the Gospel requires."

[32]See the similar story below about Anatolius.

[33]Melania appears earlier in *LH* 9. On her role, see the Introduction above.

[34]On the different figures named Isidore in early monastic literature, see J.-C. Guy, "Introduction. Prosopographie des moines scetiotes," *Apophtegmes des Pères: Collection systématique I–IX*, SC 387, 57–59.

me about the virtues of Abba Pambo, and I begged him to lead me into the desert to where Abba Pambo lived so I could see him. And when he brought me to the monastic community, *he spoke with him and took me further to the interior where he lived.*[35] *When I threw myself to the ground and prostrated myself before him, he had me sit down.* He himself was sitting and working with palm leaves. I opened my bag and gave [95] him a silver chest with three hundred silver coins inside.[36] I begged him to look inside and enjoy for himself some of my wealth. But he sat plaiting palm leaves, *absorbed in his handiwork, nor did he raise his eyes to look at me,* but instead spoke to me *in a quiet voice*: 'May the Lord bless you *for your troubles* and reward you *in heaven.' And he spoke to me again: 'Put it on the windowsill.'*

"He called Theodore,[37] his steward, and said to him, '*This woman has brought this for the stewardship of God; therefore*[38] take it and *go, spend it,* distribute it *among the monks of the Cells and* in Libya and *among the brothers living in the rocks and* on the islands, for those monasteries are poorer than all the others.' He ordered him: 'Do not distribute it among the monasteries of Egypt, because those other places,' he said, 'have more physical needs than do the ones in Egypt.'[39]

"As for me," she said, "I stood there, expecting that he would perhaps honor me or praise me, and I didn't hear a single word from

[35]This seems to suggest that Isidore took Melania to the outer part of Nitria, left her in order to speak with Pambo and get permission for her to visit, then returned for her.

[36]Coptic *lutra* for Gk *litra*, a silver coin of Sicily; as a weight, 12 ozs. (the Roman pound, *libra*), therefore 225 of our pounds, an immense weight and sum. Undoubtedly this amount will seem grossly exaggerated to us, but Melania was known for her great wealth. See, for example, *LH* 58.2, where Melania gives 300 *nomismata* to Dorotheus, who keeps three and sends the rest to Diocles because he can do a better job of distributing the money.

[37]Gk: Origen; see pars. 8, 9, and 14 below.

[38]Reading *oun* with Vogüé instead of *on*.

[39]"Egypt" probably designates the Delta or the area around Alexandria, but in Coptic monastic texts can also mean the area around Babylon (Cairo). It essentially means any place outside the monastic desert community.

him. I said to him, 'My father, [96] I wish to inform you—so you know—that there are three hundred pounds of silver there.'

"But he did not lift his head from his work but said to me in a firm voice: 'He to whom you have given them knows their number; he doesn't need anyone to weigh them for him. He who "weighs the mountains in a scale and the hills in a balance" is not ignorant of the weight of this silver [Is 40:12].[40] Indeed, if you had given the money to me, then you'd do well to inform me about it, since I am a man. But if you give the money to God, then there is no need to tell me. God, who accepted the two small coins *from the widow* [Mk 12:42], *will accept your offering too. As for yourself,* be silent; *do not boast.*'[41] *In this fashion, then, God set me at ease*[42] *and I left him.*"

And Melania said to me: "I found nothing of men in him at all."[43] *And from there she went into the great desert of Scetis and built a church for Abba Isidore the priest.*[44]

The Death of Abba Pambo (LH 10.5)

6   A few days later, Abba Pambo, the man of God, went to his rest at seventy years of age, *and no one* [97] *knew that he would die that day.* He did not have a fever but sat weaving baskets. And when he approached his last breath, it happened that Melania paid him another visit. He beckoned to her to approach and when she came to him he said to her, "Take this basket, made with the labor of my hands, in order to remember me, for I have nothing else to leave you."[45] *And then he gave his spirit into the hands of the Lord* [Ps 30:6;

[40]"Weighs," "scale," "balance," and "weight" all use *shi* in Coptic.

[41]There seems to be a play on words here: in Coptic "boast" is *shoushou* and "offering" is *shoushōoushi.*

[42]Coptic *ti mton,* "give peace, rest." The monks highly valued *mton* as a gift from God.

[43]For these last two sentences Gk has: " 'Thus,' " she said, 'did the Lord show His power when I went to the mountain.' "

[44]See Cassian, *Conferences* 18.15.3 and 7; 18.16.3.

[45]Up to here, Gk continues with Melania's narration from the previous par.

Lk 23:46]. *She directed his disciples to allow her to bury him,* and she buried him in precious linen garments. She left the desert, keeping that basket with her to the day of her death.

Abba Isidore Speaks about Abba Pambo

7   *Abba Isidore, the priest of Scetis, spoke to us about the virtues of Abba Pambo: "I begged him to lead me into the desert to where Abba Pambo lived so I could see him."*

Abba Pambo's Final Teaching (LH 10.6)

8   And these were the men, *his admirers,* who, at the hour of his departure from the body, were standing around him: Abba Macarius the priest, [98] and Abba Ammon,[46] and Abba Theodore,[47] and a multitude of leaders from among the brothers, *and they said to him, "Our father, say a word to us by which we may live."*

And the old man spoke to them thus: "From the day I came to this desert and built this cell and lived in it, I do not remember regretting a single word I've spoken[48] *or a single word that I should not have spoken, for unless I've ruminated on a word first and seen whether it is a word of death or a word of life, I have not spoken.* Nor am I aware of having eaten bread for nothing[49] without working for it with my hands [2 Th 3:8].[50] And I have not allowed myself to think

[46]= Ammonius.

[47]The Gk lists Origen, "the priest and steward," to whom Pambo addresses his final words, and Ammonius, and they do not speak.

[48]See *AP* Pambo 5 (Ward, 197).

[49]Literally "emptiness, vanity," *jinjē.* Am translates "gratis" and BV translate "gratuitement," "free of charge, for nothing."

[50]See *AP* Pambo 8, and *Life of Antony* 3.6. This sentence has a play on words: Pambo speaks of not eating and not regretting. In Coptic the former is *ouōm* while the latter is *ouōm mpahēt,* literally "eat my heart." In the next sentence, "allowed myself to think" renders *chō hen pahēt,* literally "placed it in my heart."

that I have spent a single day as a monk. Even now, as I am about to leave, I do not say that I have spent a single day serving God, but I reproach myself because I have not done the will of God."[51]

The brothers said to him, "Our father, aren't you sure that your labor and your work are of God?"

He said to them, "Up to the present I've done my best to keep the commandments, but how will I know what will happen to me when I meet God? God's judgment is one thing, human judgment is another. [99] *Mercy is his. Whatever God does with me, he does as he wishes with love. If, however, he wishes to take an accounting of me, I will not be able to be blameless before him. I do not know that I will be able to speak confidently before him."[52]*

Abba Pambo's Patience in Speaking (LH 10.7)

9   Abba Ammon and Abba Theodore and Abba Jacob[53] bore witness to us about him: If we asked for a word from Scripture or some other thing, he would not give us an answer right away but would say, "I haven't figured out the meaning[54] of this word yet; *give me two or three days to ruminate on the word and I will give you an answer.*"[55] It normally happened that he would spend two or three days or a whole week[56] without giving us an answer, saying, "If I do not know what sort of fruit this word will bear, whether it is a fruit of death[57] or of

[51]See *AP* Pambo 8; Ward, 197. Gk condenses this sentence to "and thus I go to God as one who has not even begun to serve him."

[52]Confident speaking, *parrēsia*, is an important monastic virtue. See Eph 3:12 and, for example, *AP* Pambo 14 (Ward, 198). BV accidentally omit this sentence.

[53]Gk: Origen and Ammonius.

[54]Literally "power, strength," *jom*.

[55]See *AP* Pambo 9; Ward, 197.

[56]*Synaxis*. Am translates it *hebdomade*, "week," which meaning BV point out is not attested (they transliterate the word without giving a translation), but since the synaxis usually indicated the weekly gathering of monks in a monastic community, a "week" seems likely here. Gk has "three months."

[57]Reading *phmou* with BV instead of *phōnkh*.

life, I will not speak."[58] Therefore, the brothers received the word that
he would speak as though it had come from the mouth of God.[59]

Abba Pambo Ignores a Large Sum of Money[60]

10   *Jacob, his servant,*[61] *who resembled him in every ascetic practice
except in language alone, bore witness to me: One time Anatolius the
Spaniard came to see him; he had been a secretary,* [100] *a relative of
Albinus, who was from Rome, and he had renounced the world.*[62] *He
filled a purse with gold which contained four thousand solidi and
placed it before the feet of Abba Pambo, thinking that the old man
would glorify him or be proud of him or exalt him on account of the
money. But Abba Pambo did his handiwork in silence. He did not pay
the money any attention nor did he say a word to him, and Anatolius
said to him, "My father, I have brought these necessities*[63] *to provide*[64]
for the poor."

[58]Gk: "saying that he had not comprehended it."

[59]Gk continues: "approved and shaped by His will. He is said to have excelled
even the great Antony and others in this virtue, namely, accuracy of speech."

[60]See the similar story in par. 5 above regarding Melania. This story, or the one
in par. 5, seems to have a condensed version in Socrates *EH* 4.23.

[61]BV translate "disciple," but *alou* means first a young person, then a servant. See
pars. 13–16. R.-G. Coquin has spoken of "the master and his disciple-servant," and that
seems to be the case in this *Life*. Coquin observes that at Kellia the first monastic
dwellings were for a single monk or, at the most, for a master and his disciple; these
dwellings evolved to house a number of disciples, perhaps up to a dozen. He even goes
on to assert that "the Egyptian monks scarcely conceived the anchoritic life without
the presence and aid of a companion, at one and the same time disciple and servant."
See René-Georges Coquin, "L'évolution de la vie monastique," *Dossiers Histoire et
Archéologie* [*Chrétiens d'Egypte au 4e siècle: Saint Antoine et les moines du désert*] 133
(December 1988): 60–65, at 60 and 63.

[62]In par. 14 Anatolius is a governor.

[63]Coptic *chria* = Gk *chreia* (in the plural), an unusual use here; see *LH* 67.2 and
68.2 and pars. 13, 16, and 17 below where it suggests "needs, necessities, requirements,
provisions." Am translates *chria* rather vaguely as "haec" and BV render it as "sub-
sides."

[64]*Diakonia*, which suggests both a service or provision of money, and a ministry
of charitable service; see Lampe 351A (A2) and 351B (B5b).

The old man said to him, "I already know that, my son."

Anatolius said to him, "But I want you to know how much it is."

The old man said, "That which you have brought has no need[65] for you to recount its number."

Therefore Anatolius placed the money before him and left. He spoke to the priests, "My soul has not profited from this large amount of money I brought as much as it has from the disposition and self-possession of the old man. He treated me as though I'd brought him one *solidus!"*

Abba Pambo's Good Works and Humility

11   *Abba Pambo was admired* [101] *by the whole brotherhood and by the laity as well[66] for his good works and for the magnitude of his humility.[67]*

Abba Pambo Learns from a Prostitute[68]

12   *They also said concerning him that Abba Athanasius sent for him one time and had him brought to Alexandria. When he entered the city he saw a woman of the theater adorned with finery. Immediately his eyes filled with tears. Therefore, when the brothers who were with him saw him, they said to him, "Our father, we beg you, tell us what caused these tears."*

---

[65]*Chria.* See n. 63 above.

[66]Adding *nem nikekosmikos on* with Vogüé.

[67]This is a common monastic usage, which speaks often of "the heights of humility." In addition, the phrase looks back to the story about Anatolius. The "large amount" of money that he brought, which gained him no special respect in Pambo's eyes, translates Coptic *ashai,* the same word rendered here by "magnitude."

[68]See *AP* Pambo 4 (Ward, 196). See also Socrates *EH* 4.23. In the *Life of Pelagia* 3–4 the same story is told concerning Bishop Nonnus when he sees Pelagia pass by in Antioch.

He said to them, "Two things move me at this moment: one is the destruction of this soul that I see now; the other is my own ungrateful soul which, in adorning itself with the virtues and in pleasing the Lord and his angels, does not even have the appearance or the finery of this prostitute."

The Faithful Disciple

13   He had a disciple who was very faithful in taking care of necessities. It was revealed to him by God that he loved the curse of Gehazi, the servant of the prophet Elisha [2 Kings 5:19b–27][69]

Origen the Steward

14   Abba Pambo took[70] the money of the governor Anatolius and gave it to his servant [102] named Origen,[71] who is still living and performing the job of steward that the old man gave him.

We Work for What We Eat and Wear[72]

15   He gloried in the Lord while telling us numerous times, "Neither I nor my servants are aware of eating a single piece of bread given to us by someone else without working for it with our hands, nor have we clothed ourselves through the labor of strangers without working for it ourselves."

---

[69]Gehazi deceptively takes money from Naaman. When Elisha confronts him, he lies, and Elisha curses him and his descendants with leprosy.

[70]Reading *el* with Vogüé instead of *jel*.

[71]See the Introduction above.

[72]See par. 8 above and *AP* Pambo 8.

Giving to Others

16   *He would also do this other thing: he gave nothing for the service*[73] *of servants unless it was to an old man, poor and infirm, who was unable to acquire bread for himself. Moreover, with regard to the monks who lived there, he did not give them anything from the provisions*[74] *he had at hand but instead chose for himself ten faithful brothers whom he sent to the islands and to Libya each year*[75] *and to the lepers' colony in Alexandria; loading the boats with grain and bread, they would distribute them to those in need*[76] *and also to the churches of villages that were in need*[77] *and to the churches of the interior deserts in barbarian territory.*

I tell you this so you (pl.) will understand why he did not give anything to the monks who lived there. Seek and you (sing.) will understand that he began a custom among the brothers who lived in [103] *Egypt and Pernouj: each one would give an artaba*[78] *of grain per person each year and they would put them at the service*[79] *of those in need,*[80] *distributing them to the hospices for lepers and to the widows and orphans* [Dt 14:29, Is 1:17, and Jas 1:27]. *Each of the monks would have the responsibility each year to give the artaba of grain from his charitable labor,*[81] *and this is their custom up to today.*

---

[73]*Diakonia.*
[74]*Chria.* See notes 63 and 65.
[75]See par. 5 above.
[76]*Chria.*
[77]*Chria.*
[78]Coptic *ertob* comes from the Persian by way of Gk *artabē*, a measure ranging from 24 to 42 *choinikes*, roughly equivalent to English quarts. A *choinix* of grain was considered one person's daily allowance.
[79]*Diakonia.*
[80]*Chria.*
[81]*Hise nagapē*, literally "labor of love." *Agapē*, "love," also came to designate fraternal charity, an act of charity, almsgiving; see Lampe, 8A–B.

Abba Pambo Teaches Abba Pihor a Lesson (LH 10.8)

17   In addition, this *other wondrous* story is told about our father, *Saint Apa* Pambo: *Apa* Pihor the ascetic, *the disciple of Abba Antony,* wanted to pay him a visit one time.[82] He had his bread with him *and two olives so he could go see him.* Apa Pambo said to him, "What are these things, Pihor?"

Apa Pihor said to him, "I decided to stay one day with you; therefore I've brought a few necessities[83] with me."[84]

The old man in his wisdom understood that Pihor had vowed not to eat another person's bread,[85] *so later* Abba Pambo wanted to teach him *not to maintain his desire* [104] *when he went to see the old men.* Apa Pambo *got up and* paid a visit *in turn* to Apa Pihor. He moistened his bread before he went to see him *and also [took]*[86] *a bottle of water.*

When he entered Apa Pihor's dwelling, Apa Pihor said to him, "My father, what are these things?"[87]

The old man said to him,[88] "It's my bread and my water. So I won't trouble you, I moistened my bread before coming to see you."

Apa Pambo did this in order to silently teach him a lesson.[89]

---

[82]On Pior or Pihor, see Evelyn White, 2.51–52.

[83]*Chria.*

[84]For this sentence Gk has "So that I need not bother you."

[85]See pars. 8 and 15 above.

[86]The verb, missing in Coptic, is supplied by Am and BV.

[87]Adding with Vogüé *paiōt* at the beginning of the question and omitting *pamō* at the end.

[88]Reading *pihello* with Vogüé instead of *apa pamō.*

[89]Gk puts this sentence earlier and adds "very forcefully."

CHAPTER TWO

The Life of Evagrius
(*Lausiac History* 38)

INTRODUCTION

The Coptic Life of Evagrius[1]

There are two chief, and very important, differences between the *Life of Evagrius* as presented in the *Lausiac History* and in the Coptic *Life*: first, the Coptic *Life* is considerably longer. Put another way, the version found in the *Lausiac History* is considerably shorter, probably due to anti-Origenistic editorial pruning (for a full discussion, see the General Introduction).[2] Second, the version in the *Lausiac History* mostly chronicles *events* and is concerned more with Evagrius' early life and how he came to Egypt while the Coptic *Life* includes these events but enriches them with much more detail about Evagrius' *interior* life. Reading about Evagrius in the *Lausiac History*, one is surprised, and disappointed, that someone like Palladius, who knew Evagrius, would be so superficial about this great desert theologian of prayer; the account seems to be one that a more distant observer, say the Church historian Socrates, might write. As Gabriel

---

[1]For a discussion of Evagrius, his situation at Scetis, and the issue of the Coptic *Life* vis-à-vis the *Lausiac History* of Palladius, see the Introduction to this volume.

[2]As C.P. Bammel has observed, "Problems of the *Historia Monachorum*," 100, the section on Evagrius in the *Historia Monachorum* is "much shorter in the Greek than the Latin and omits some of the praises included in the Latin version."

Bunge has observed, with regard to Evagrius the Greek *Lausiac History* "is astonishingly colorless, which is even more peculiar because Palladius lived nearly ten years as an intimate of Evagrius."[3] The Coptic *Life of Evagrius* is much more what one would have expected from Palladius: much more of an exploration of the way of life in the desert, about the one "who taught me the way of life in Christ and he who helped me understand Holy Scripture spiritually" (par. 2); as Bunge notes, its pages "are particularly rich in concrete and specific details which one would not seriously suggest have been purely and simply invented."[4] Thus, if the Coptic *Life of Evagrius* represents an eyewitness account from the fourth century (see par. 2), as seems likely, then it is precious testimony indeed to a small part of the origins and first rich flowering of Christian monasticism.

The *Life of Evagrius* followed that of Pambo in the Coptic synaxary and was read on the fifth Sunday of Lent.

[3]Gabriel Bunge, "Évagre le Pontique et les deux Macaires," 324.
[4]Bunge, "Évagre le Pontique," 325.

SYNOPTIC TABLE

The Coptic *Life of Evagrius & Lausiac History* 38

Coptic *Life*	*Lausiac History*
1. Prologue	*LH* 38.1
2. Palladius Testifies as an Eyewitness	—
3. Palladius' Own Testimony	—
4. Evagrius' Origins and Early Years	*LH* 38.2
5. Evagrius Lusts after a Married Woman	*LH* 38.3
6. Angels Appear to Arrest Evagrius	*LH* 38.4
7. An Angel Visits Evagrius Disguised as a Friend	*LH* 38.5–7
8. Evagrius Goes to Melania but Lapses and Becomes Ill	*LH* 38.8
9. Evagrius Confesses, Heals, and Leaves for Egypt	*LH* 38.9
10. Evagrius Goes to the Cells and Remains There	*LH* 38.10
11. Evagrius Asks Abba Macarius about Fornication	—
12. Evagrius' Advanced Asceticism	*LH* 38.10
13. Evagrius' Strict Ascetic Regimen	*LH* 38.12–13
14. Evagrius' Contemplative Practices	—
15. Evagrius' Gifts	*LH* 38.10
16. Evagrius' Fidelity to the Church, and His Writings	—
17. Evagrius the Spiritual Director	—
18. Evagrius' Hospitality	—
19. Evagrius Refuses to be Ordained	—
20. Demons Attack Evagrius	—
21. The Book He Wrote about Them	—
22. The Demon of Fornication Attacks Evagrius	*LH* 38.11
23. The Spirit of Blasphemy Attacks Him	*LH* 38.11
24. Evagrius' Mystical Ascent	—
25. Evagrius Teaches about Humility	—
26. The Purity of His Language	—
27. Evagrius Saves a Tribune's Wife in Palestine	—
28. Discerning Good and Evil Events	—
29. Evagrius' Encounter with Demons in Disguise	[*LH* 38.11][5]

[5]The version in *LH* 38.11 is much shorter than that found in the Coptic *Life*; see the discussion in the General Introduction to this volume.

The Life of Evagrius[6]

Prologue (LH 38.1)[7]

1   [104] I will now also begin to speak about Apa Evagrius, the deacon *from Constantinople, upon whom the bishop Gregory laid hands.*[8]
Indeed, it is right that we relate the virtues of him whom everyone
praises: he lived the apostolic way of life. For it would not be just if
we were silent about his progress and ‹works› acceptable to God;[9]
[105] rather, it is right that we put them into writing for the edifica-
tion and profit of those who read about them so they may glorify
God our Savior who empowers human beings to do these things.

Palladius Testifies as an Eyewitness[10]

2   *Indeed, it was also he who taught me the way of life in Christ and
he who helped me understand Holy Scripture spiritually*[11] *and told me*

---

[6]Translated from the text edited by É. Amélineau, *De Historia Lausica, quaenam
sit huius ad Monachorum Aegyptiorum historiam scribendam utilitas* (Paris, 1887):
92–104, with important corrections by Adalbert de Vogüé, based on Vatican Coptic
Codex 64, "Les fragments coptes de l'Histoire Lausiaque: l'édition d'Amélineau et le
manuscrit," *Orientalia*, 58.3 (1989): 326–32. Numbers in brackets give the pagination
of Amélineau's text. Gabriel Bunge and Vogüé give a French translation of the corrected text. References to the Greek [Gk] text of the *Lausiac History* are to G. J. M.
Bartelink, ed., *Palladio: La Storia Lausiaca* (Milan: Fondazione Lorenzo Valla, 1974),
which is a modification of Butler's. Translations of the Gk text are from *Palladius: The
Lausiac History*, trans. Robert T. Meyer (ACW 34; New York: Newman, 1964).

[7]Section titles and paragraphing are my own. Portions in italics are lacking in Gk.
Paragraphs without "*LH*" in parentheses lack parallels with the *Lausiac History*. Paragraph numbers do not correspond to *LH* but are given for ease of reference.

[8]BV suggest that the editor amalgamated the preambles of two redactions.

[9]Following BV's emendation of *enefh‹b›ēoui*. "Acceptable" renders *shenho* (Crum
648B); I have followed BV in adding "to God."

[10]On the disciple-master relationship with Evagrius, see *LH* 23.1 (Meyer, 81),
where Palladius calls Evagrius "my teacher," and Socrates *EH* 4.23. In *Epistle* 51.1 Evagrius calls Palladius his "brother." According to the *LH*, Palladius arrived in Kellia in
390–91, well after Evagrius, who came there around 383 [BV].

[11]That is, allegorically. For Evagrius as a biblical commentator, see Paul Géhin,

what old wives' tales are [1 Tim 4:7][12] *in order that, as it is written, sin might be revealed as a sinner* [Rom 7:13], *for the whole time I was in that monastic settlement*[13] *I was with him, each*[14] *of us living enclosed and apart. I was by his side Saturday night and during the day on Sunday.*[15] *In order that someone not think that I am praising him or showing favoritism towards him, as Christ is my witness I saw the majority of his virtues with my own eyes as well as the wonders that he performed.*[16] *These I will write down for you for the profit of those who will read about them and for those who will hear them read so they will glorify Christ who gives power to his poor*[17] *to do what is pleasing to him.*

Palladius' Own Testimony

3   *I myself have been deemed worthy to inform you how he lived, from the beginning of his life until he arrived at these measures and these great ascetic practices until* [106] *he completed sixty years,*[18] *and in this way went to his rest, as it is written, "In a short period of time he completed a multitude of years"* [Wis 4:13].[19]

Évagre le Pontique: Scholies aux Proverbes (SC 340; Paris: Cerf, 1987), and Géhin, *Évagre le Pontique: Scholies à l'Ecclésiaste* (SC 397; Paris: Cerf, 1993). Evagrius' *Scholia on the Psalms* are found scattered among the works of Origen: PG 12:1053–1686; an edition is forthcoming.

[12]"Old wives' tales" means "false knowledge," of which Evagrius often speaks in his letters.

[13]Or: on the mountain (*tōou*).

[14]Adding *piouai* after *piouai* with Vogüé.

[15]At Kellia the monks would live by themselves during the week and come together on Saturday (the Sabbath) and Sunday (the Lord's day) for communal meals, worship, and the celebration of the Eucharist.

[16]Adding with Vogüé after *ainau erōou nnabal nem nijom etafaitou.*

[17]"The poor" (*ebiain*) became a monastic self-designation; see Paul of Tamma, *On the Cell*; Tim Vivian and Birger A. Pearson, "Saint Paul of Tamma on the Monastic Cell (de Cella)," *Hallel*, 23.2 (1998): 86–107; 92.

[18]According to *LH* 38.1 Evagrius lived to be only 54. The number 60 is repeated below.

[19]This quotation is repeated by Palladius in *Dialogue* 20, which suggests the Palladian origins of this material; see Robert T. Meyer, trans., *Palladius: Dialogue on the Life of St. John Chrysostom* (ACW 45; New York and Mahwah: Newman, 1985), 141–42.

Evagrius' Origins and Early Years (LH 38.2)

4   This man of whom we speak was a citizen of Pontus, which is
where his family was from. He was the son of a priest from Iberia[20]
whom the blessed Basil, bishop of Cappadocia, had made a priest *for
the church in Arkeus.*[21] After the death of Saint Basil the bishop, and
his father in God the priest,[22] Evagrius went to Constantinople, a
city filled with learning,[23] for he walked in the footsteps of Saint
Basil. He attached himself to Gregory [of Nazianzus], the bishop of
Constantinople,[24] and when the bishop saw his learning and good
intelligence, he made him a deacon, *for truly he was a wise person,
being in possession of himself and without passions,*[25] *and was a deacon of steadfast character.*[26] Indeed, he himself attended [the Coun-

[20]Gk reads Ibora, a place in Helenopontus, a town in Cappadocia not far from
the monastery of Saint Basil of Caesarea; see Sozomen *EH* 3.30 [Meyer, 200 n. 339];
Jerome *Epistle* 133 (CSEL 56.246), speaks of "*euagrius ponticus hiborita.*" BV point out,
154 n. 9, that Ibora and Iberia were commonly confused in antiquity. However, it
should be noted that there were two Iberias: the Spanish peninsula and the land
(roughly coinciding with modern Georgia) south of the Caucasus, northeast of
Armenia, between the Black Sea and the Caspian Sea. Thus Iberia was in fact near
Pontus.

[21]In the Gk, Basil ordains Evagrius as a lector and the Gk text does not mention
Arkeus; Basil is identified as "bishop of the church of Caesarea," not Cappadocia, and
one wonders if "Arkeus" is a corruption of Caesarea; the more general term "Cappadocia" would have been more familiar to a Coptic audience.

[22]According to Evagrius' letters, his father died when he was in the desert [BV].
Gk does not mention his father's death. A "father in God" normally designates a spiritual father, an abba, rather than a parent.

[23]Or: doctrine, *sbō.*

[24]Both *LH* 38.2 and Socrates *EH* 4.23 affirm that it was Gregory of Nazianazus.
In *Praktikos,* Epilogue (Bamberger, 42), Evagrius refers to Gregory as "the just Gregory who planted me." In *Gnostikos* 44 he again refers to Gregory as "the just."

[25]Reading *nnipathos* with Vogüé instead of *nnipothos.* Gk identifies Gregory as
being of Nazianzus and omits "for truly ... character." "Without passions" anticipates
Evagrius' later ascetic life. *Apatheia* is a key term in Evagrius' spiritual vocabulary and
Palladius' use of it is a signal he knows Evagrian terminology. The best discussion of
"apatheia" in Evagrius is Antoine Guillaumont, "Introduction: (6) L'impassibilite," in
Évagre le Pontique: Traité pratique ou le moine (SC 170; Paris: Cerf, 1971), 98–112.

[26]Sozomen *EH* 6.30, describes him as "archdeacon," that is, the right-hand man
of the bishop, who often enough was chosen as the bishop's successor.

cil of] Constantinople with our fathers the bishops at the time of the synod that took place in Constantinople, and he was victorious over all the heretics. Thus this Evagrius and Nectarius [107] the bishop debated with each other face to face, for truly Evagrius was very protective of the Scriptures and was well equipped to refute every heresy[27] with his wisdom.[28] He was therefore well known throughout[29] Constantinople for having combated the heretics with forceful and eloquent language.

Evagrius Lusts after a Married Woman (LH 38.3)

5   The whole city praised him greatly.[30] After all this learning [. . .][31] on account of his pride and arrogance, he fell into the hands *of the demon* who brings about lustful thoughts for women,[32] as he told us later after he had been freed from this passion. Indeed, the woman loved him very much in return. But Evagrius was fearful before God and did not sin with her because, *in fact, the woman was married*[33] and Evagrius also followed his conscience *because her husband was a member of the nobility and greatly honored*[34] and, fur-

[27]Reading *nniheresis* with Vogüé instead of *nniheretikos*.

[28]The Coptic translator has mistakenly turned Nectarius, bishop of Constantinople from 381–97, into one of the (Arian) heretics. Gk says that Gregory entrusted Evagrius to Nectarius, "one most skillful in confuting all heresies."

[29]Adding *tērs* with Vogüé.

[30]The attentive Coptic reader or listener might have heard that the verb used here for "praise," *ti ōou*, is the same as that used at the end of par. 1 where glory (*ōou*) is given to God. Thus, as will be immediately evident, glory, laud, and honor are misplaced here, given to the creature rather than to the Creator. Like a figure in classical Greek drama, Evagrius will pay for his hubris, "his pride and arrogance" (par. 5). See n. 120 below.

[31]The text, *chouōsh*, is corrupt.

[32]Gk does not mention a demon, but rather the thought. It is interesting that the Coptic adds the demon since Evagrius in his writings so painstakingly delineated the various demons and their corresponding passions and often used "thought" and "demon" interchangeably. See pars. 15 and 22.

[33]Sozomen *EH* 6.29, also reports that she was married.

[34]Gk does not mention the husband but says simply that "she was of the highest social class."

thermore, Evagrius thought deeply about the magnitude of shame and sin and judgment and realized that all the ‹heretics›[35] whom he had humiliated would rejoice. He beseeched God continuously, praying that he help free him from the passion and warfare that he had been subjected to,[36] for in truth the woman persisted in [108] ‹her›[37] madness for him to the point that she made a public spectacle of herself.[38] He wanted to flee from her but could not summon up the courage to do so for in truth his thoughts were held captive by pleasure *like a child.*

Angels Appear to Arrest Evagrius (LH 38.4)

6   God's mercy did not delay in coming to him but through his entreaties and prayers[39] God came to him quickly. He comforted him[40] through a revelation so that nothing evil could get at him with the woman.[41] In a vision *at night,* the Lord sent angels to him *dressed in radiant clothing*[42] who looked like soldiers of the prefect. They made him stand and seized him as though they were taking him before a judge, as though they had bound him in ropes along with other thieves, having put a collar around his neck and chains on his feet,[43] acting as though they were arresting him but without telling him the charges or why they had seized him.[44] But he thought in his heart that they had come after him on account of the affair with the

[35]Emending *niheresis* (which Am marks with [*sic*]) to *niheretikos*; BV leave as "heresies." Gk has "heretics."

[36]"that . . . him": Gk "to God to put some impediment in his path." For "continuously" Gk has "humbly."

[37]Reading *peslibi* instead of *peflibi.*

[38]Reading *srah* with Vogüé instead of *sroh.*

[39]Reading *neftōbh* with Vogüé instead of *teftōbh.*

[40]*Ti nomti* literally means "give strength, power, encouragement, comfort." *Reftinomti* is Coptic for the Comforter.

[41]Gk simplifies this sentence to "After he had been at prayer a short time."

[42]Reading *hebsō* with Vogüé instead of *sbō.*

[43]Gk: tied his hands; see Sozomen *EH* 6.30.

[44]Gk simplifies the sentence to "They did not tell him why."

woman, thinking that [109] her husband had accused him before the prefect.[45]

An Angel Visits Evagrius Disguised as a Friend (LH 38.5–7)

7   Afterwards he was utterly astonished,[46] and the angel who had appeared to him changed form in front of him, taking on the appearance of one of his friends[47] who had come to pay him a visit and comfort him. He said to Evagrius, who was bound with the thieves,[48] "Deacon Evagrius, why have you been arrested, sir?"

Evagrius said to him, "The truth is, I don't know, but I think someone denounced me, perhaps because he was seized by ignorant jealousy. So I'm afraid that he's given money to the judge so he will quickly and violently destroy me."

The angel said to him, "If you will listen to me, who am your friend, then I will tell you: It is not good for you to stay in this city."

Evagrius said to him, "If God delivers me from this trouble and you still see me in this city of Constantinople, say 'You deserve this punishment.' "[49]

The angel who had taken on the appearance of a friend said to him,[50] "I will give you the Gospel; swear to me 'I will not remain in this city,' and that you will be concerned about the salvation of your soul. I will save you [110] from this trouble."[51]

And he swore to him upon the Gospel, "Give me one day to load[52] my clothes on the boat and I swear to you[53] I will leave this city."

---

[45]Coptic "had accused him before the prefect": Gk "had brought this about."

[46]Coptic lacks "for another trial was going on with others being tried for some complaint or other."

[47]Gk: a genuine friend.

[48]Gk: forty criminals.

[49]"Say ... punishment": Gk "know that I would undergo this punishment without complaint."

[50]Gk: "Then the vision spoke."

[51]Reading *taianagkē* with Vogüé instead of *taiagapē*.

[52]Reading *shatitalo* with Vogüé instead of *shatialo*.

[53]Adding *mmon*, literally "truly," with Vogüé.

After he had sworn, he awoke from the vision he had seen at night and said, "Even if I swore in a dream, nevertheless I have sworn this oath."[54] He immediately got up, loaded his things and his clothes on the boat, and set sail for Jerusalem.

Evagrius Goes to Melania but Lapses and Becomes Ill (LH 38.8)

8   Blessed Melania the Roman joyfully welcomed him. But once again the Devil hardened his heart as in the time of Pharaoh [Ex 7:14], and his heart doubted and became divided; and on account of his boiling youthfulness and his very learned speech, and because of his large and splendid wardrobe (he would change clothes *twice a day*), he fell into vain habits *and bodily pleasure.* But God, who always keeps destruction from his people, sent a tempest of fever and chills[55] upon him until he contracted a grave illness that persisted until his flesh became as thin as thread.[56]

Evagrius Confesses, Heals, and Leaves for Egypt (LH 38.9)

9   [111] This illness afflicted him with every sort of hidden suffering[57] so that the doctors were perplexed and were unable to cure him. Saint Melania said to him, "Evagrius, my child, this persistent illness does not please me. Do not hide your thoughts from me; perhaps I will be able to cure you. Tell me your thoughts in all honesty, for I can see by looking at you that this illness has not come over you without God's permission."[58] Then he revealed all his thoughts to her.[59] She said to him, "Give me your word that you will take the

---

[54]Reading *mpianash* with Vogüé instead of *mpianaf.*

[55]Gk: a six-month fever.

[56]A nice image. "Which . . . thread": Gk "This wasted away his flesh which had been his great impediment."

[57]Evagrius' physical suffering (*pipathos*) is a direct result of his fleshly passions (*nipathos*).

[58]"Perhaps . . . permission": Gk "for your sickness is not beyond God's aid."

[59]Gk: Then he confessed the whole story.

monastic habit and, although I am a sinner, I will entreat my God through his grace to make you whole." He gave her his word and after a few days he was healthy again. He arose and took the monastic habit[60] and left. He walked and came to the monastic settlement of Pernouj,[61] which is in Egypt.

Evagrius Goes to the Cells and Remains There (LH 38.10)

10   And he remained there two years and the third year he left there and went to the desert of the Cells.[62] He remained there sixteen years,[63] undertaking there numerous ascetic practices,[64] *and he went to his rest[65] at sixty years of age. He did not see the* [112] *bitterness of the body's old age and thus went to his rest as it is written: "In a short while he completed many years and he was quickly taken to the Lord so that evil might not alter his understanding."*[66]

Evagrius Asks Abba Macarius about Fornication[67]

11   *One day he asked our father Abba Macarius,*[68] *"My father, how will I be able to oppose the spirit of fornication?"*[69]

[60]The Gk emphasizes that Evagrius "received a change of clothing at her hands." According to Evagrius, *Epistle* 22.1, it was Rufinus who clothed Evagrius in the monastic habit [BV].

[61]That is, Nitria, some 50 kilometers southeast of Alexandria.

[62]Gk lacks "of the Cells" here and places "the so-called Kellia" in the next sentence. Kellia (Cells) was about 18 kilometers south of Nitria.

[63]Gk: fourteen.

[64]Gk specifies: "eating but a pound of bread and a pint of oil in the space of three months, and he was a man who had been delicately reared in a refined and fastidious manner of life." Gk lacks the rest of this sentence, and the remainder of the paragraph is completely different.

[65]Reading *mmof* with Vogüé instead of *mmau.*

[66]See Wisd 4:11, 13 and par. 3 above.

[67]For a similar visit by Evagrius to Macarius, see *Virtues of Macarius* 42 (in the companion volume to this one, *Saint Macarius the Spiritbearer*).

[68]Adding *abba* with Vogüé.

[69]In the *Life of Antony* 6.2, the Devil tells Antony he is "the friend of fornication."

The old man said to him, "Do not eat anything in order to be filled up, neither fruit nor anything cooked over a fire."[70]

Evagrius' Advanced Asceticism (LH 38.10)

12   He was a person to admire, having left behind a life of ease and pleasure, *and he did not*[71] *judge anyone, so that we recognized his maturity from the beginning.* He said one hundred prayers a day, while being a very skilled scribe.[72]

---

[70]In *Praktikos* 94 (Bamberger, p. 40) "the holy Father Macarius" tells Evagrius, "For twenty years I have not taken my fill of bread or water or sleep. I have eaten my bread by scant weight, and drunk my water by measure, and snatched a few winks of sleep while leaning against a wall." Evagrius counseled monks never to eat or sleep to satiety; since one passion (gluttony) could lead to another (lust), such restraint was part of the monastic effort to reduce sexual desire. For Evagrius (and for Poemen and many other Desert Fathers), gluttony was the first sin, the first sin of Adam, and from it all others flowed. In the *Apophthegmata* there is the frequent admonition to "guard your belly"; fasting is the first step in undoing the sin of Adam. For Evagrius, failure to control one's food opened oneself to lust: "It is not possible to fall into the hands of the spirit of fornication if one has not fallen under the blows of [the spirit] of gluttony," *De diversis malignis cogitationibus* 1 (PG 79:1200–1201). On all this, see A. and C. Guillaumont, "Introduction," in *Évagre le Pontique: Le Traité pratique ou le Moine* (SC 170–71; Paris: Cerf, 1971), 90–93. See also Evagrius, *De jejunio* 8; J. Muyldermans, ed. and trans., *Evagriana Syriaca: Textes inédits du British Museum et de la Vaticane* (Louvain: Publications Universitaires/Institut Orientaliste, 1952), Syriac 116, French 151, and Evagrius, *De diversis malignis cogitationibus* 1 (PG 79.1200). If this account is accurate, Evagrius learned the connection between gustatory and sexual appetites from Macarius. See Guillaumont, "Évagre le Pontique et les deux Macaires."

[71]Reading *an* with Vogüé instead of *on*.

[72]Gk: "He composed one hundred prayers, and he wrote during the year only the price of as much as he ate, for he wrote very gracefully the Oxyrhynchus character." Coptic lacks the rest of Gk *LH* 38.10 which speaks of Evagrius' spiritual gifts and of the three books he wrote. One hundred "prayers" would be a "century," a form that Evagrius liked to use and apparently a title that Evagrius used for the *Praktikos*; see A. and C. Guillaumont, eds., *Traité Pratique ou le Moine*, 384–86. Gk 38.11 occurs much later in the Coptic version; see pars. 22–23, 29 below.

Evagrius' Strict Ascetic Regimen (LH 38.12–13)

13   At the end of nearly eight years[73] of keeping a stringent regimen of ascetic practice without relaxing it at all, he managed to damage his bowels and because the food he ate was like stones his bladder[74] hurt him.[75] The elders had him change his ascetic regimen and thus he did not eat bread until the day he died but would eat a few [113] herbs and a little cooked barley,[76] which proved sufficient for him until he spent his little bit of time.[77] As for fruit or anything else that gives the body pleasure, he did not eat them nor did he allow his servants to eat them.[78] This was his ascetic regimen with regard to food.

Evagrius' Contemplative Practices

14   *With regard to sleep, he followed a rule: he would sleep a third of the night, but during the day he would not sleep at all.[79] He had a*

[73]Gk: sixteenth year.

[74]Reading *pefma* with Vogüé instead of *ma*. Crum, 263B, suggests that *pefma nphen mōou ebol nhemsi* = "anus, rectum (?)." *Phen mōou* means "urinate"; thus "bladder" seems like a reasonable translation here. But *ma nhemsi* means "anus," so perhaps both Evagrius' rectum and his bladder hurt him.

[75]Gk says that as a result "his body required food prepared over a fire." In the *Life of Antony* 61.1, "Polycratia, a remarkable Christ-bearing young woman in Laodicea ... suffered terribly with pain in her stomach and side on account of her excessive asceticism and her whole body was weakened." On the subject of food permitted to sick monks, see Lucien Regnault, *La vie quotidienne des pères du désert en Égypte au IVe siècle* (Paris: Hachette, 1990), chapter 6, "Le Régime alimentaire," 75–94, esp. 85–87.

[76]Following BV's suggestion that *sisani* = Gk *ptisanē*. Theodoret, *Religious History* 21.11, reports that a sick monk eats some *ptisanē*; see R. M. Price, trans., *A History of the Monks of Syria* (Kalamazoo: Cistercian, 1985), 137.

[77]Gk lacks the intervention of the elders at the beginning of this sentence and at the end says that "he died after having communicated in the church at Epiphany."

[78]Gk: He said: "I did not touch lettuce or any vegetable greens, or fruit, or grapes, nor did I even take a bath, since the time I came to the desert." Although BV believe this sentence corresponds to *LH* 38.12, it is so different that there may be no connection.

[79]A third of the night was four hours; the other two-thirds were devoted to the office and work. This "rule" was apparently common at Kellia (BV).

courtyard where he would spend the middle part of each day walking,[80]
driving away sleep from himself, training his intellect to examine his
thoughts systematically.[81] *When he had finished sleeping a third of the*
night, he would spend the rest of the night walking in the courtyard,
meditating[82] *and praying, driving sleep away from himself, training*
his intellect to reflect on the meaning of the Scriptures.[83]

Evagrius' Gifts (LH 38.10)

15   He possessed a very pure intelligence and[84] was deemed worthy
to receive the gift[85] of wisdom and knowledge and discernment,[86]
with which he categorized the works of the demons.[87]

Evagrius' Fidelity to the Church and His Writings

16   *And he was very scrupulous with regard to the Holy Scriptures and*
the orthodox traditions of the Catholic Church. Indeed, [114] *the books*

[80]On the architecture of the cells uncovered in Kellia, see Myriam Orban, ed.,
Déserts chrétiens d'Égypte (Nice: Culture Sud, 1993), with photos of the excavations at
Kellia, and Georges Descoeudres, "L'architecture des ermitages et des sanctuaires," in
Les Kellia: Ermitages coptes en Basse-Egypte (Geneva: Musée d'art et d'histoire, 1990),
33–55.

[81]Columba Stewart, "Imageless Prayer," 185 n. 50, makes the intriguing suggestion that Coptic *etsmont*, "systematically," could have originally been *atsmont*, "form-
less"; thus Evagrius would have been training his thoughts to be imageless (see the
discussion in the General Introduction above). As Stewart concludes, "Despite the
lack of extant manuscript support for this possibility, it is a tempting speculation
given Evagrius' teaching on prayer."

[82]Coptic/Gk *meletē* meant to meditate on Scripture, that is, to quietly utter on
one's lips the words of Scripture, most commonly the Psalms. See n. 101 below.

[83]On nocturnal vigils, see Evagrius *Ad monachos* 46–51 and *Antirrhetikos* II.55
(BV).

[84]Gk: "Within fifteen years he had so purified his mind that he."

[85]Or grace, *hmot*: Gk *charisma*.

[86]Gk: discernment of spirits. A very important trait in the *Life of Antony*.

[87]A reference to the *Praktikos*?

*he wrote testify to his teaching and knowledge and remarkable intelli-
gence. For he wrote three books of teaching:*[88] *one concerning the cenobitic monks, another concerning the monks who lived in cells in the
desert, and another concerning the priests of God in order for them to
be vigilant with regard to their duties in the sanctuary. These three
works teach everyone to live a good life, to possess a firm understanding, and to have an orthodox way of seeing things according to the traditions of the Church.*[89]

Evagrius the Spiritual Director[90]

17 *This was his practice: The brothers would gather around him on
Saturday and Sunday, discussing their thoughts with him throughout
the night, listening to his words of encouragement until sunrise. And
thus they would leave rejoicing and glorifying God, for Evagrius' teaching was very sweet.*[91] *When they came to see him, he encouraged them,
saying to them, "My brothers, if one of you has either a profound or a
troubled thought, let him be silent until the brothers depart and let him
reflect on it alone with me. Let us not make him speak* [115] *in front of*

[88]Or doctrine, *sbō.*

[89]What are these "three works"? The one to the cenobites may be *Ad monachos*,
the one to the solitaries *Praktikos*, but there are a number that could fit this category;
it is not clear what the one concerning priests could be. Evagrius very rarely speaks
about the eucharist; see *Gnostikos* 14. *LH* 38.10 condenses Evagrius' writings thusly
(partly seen in the last sentence of par. 16 above): "Then he drew up three holy books
for monks—Controversies [or Refutations: *Antirrhētika*] they are called—on the arts
to be used against demons." It is interesting that Evagrius' works are so often listed in
threes: In his *Epistle to Ctesiphon* (CSEL 56.246), Jerome says that Evagrius wrote to
virgins, monks, and to Melania. Evagrius, in his letter to Anatolius (PG 40.1221), seems
to refer to the *Praktikos*, *Gnostikos*, and *Kephalaia Gnostika.*

[90]See *LH* 26.1 and [73.4] (Appendix II below) and the letter from Abba Lucius to
Evagrius preserved in Arabic, with a French translation, in Irenée Hausherr, "Eulo-
gios-Loukios," *Orientalia Christiana Periodica* 6 (1940): 216–20 [BV].

[91]Sweetness was the essence of Evagrius' spiritual teaching and personality and
is also an important word in the "Life of Macarius of Scetis" (in the companion volume to this one, *Saint Macarius the Spiritbearer*); see G. Bunge, *Evagrios Pontikos:
Briefe aus der Wüste* (Trier, 1986), 70ff., 126 ff.; *AP* Evagrius 7; Sozomen *EH* 6.30.

*the brothers lest a little one perish on account of his thoughts and grief
swallow him at a gulp."*

Evagrius' Hospitality

18   *Furthermore, he was so hospitable that his cell never lacked five or
six visitors a day who had come from foreign lands to listen to his teaching, his intellect, and his ascetic practice.*[92] *As a result, he had money
because in truth large numbers of people would send it to him. You
would find more than two hundred coins in his possession which he
would entrust to his steward who served in his house at all times.*[93]

Evagrius Refuses to be Ordained

19   *Numerous times Apa Theophilus the archbishop wished to take
him and make him bishop of Thmoui,*[94] *but he would not agree to this
and fled from the archbishop so he could not ordain him.*[95]

Demons Attack Evagrius

20   *One time the demons paid him a visit and wounded him several
times. We heard their voices but did not see them.*[96] *They struck him at
night with ox-hide whips and, as God is our witness, we saw with our
own eyes the wounds they inflicted on his body.*

---

[92]In his letters Evagrius himself often speaks of such visitors and the letters he
received; see *Ep.* 10.1, 22.1 [BV].

[93]See the interesting parallels in *Life of Pambo* 5 and 10 above.

[94]Thmuis, an important city in the Delta.

[95]Evagrius seems to refer to this in *Ep.* 13; see also Socrates *EH* 4.23 [BV].

[96]See *Life of Antony* 13.

The Book He Wrote about Them

21   If you [sing.] want to know the experiences that he underwent at the hands of the demons, read the book he wrote concerning the suggestions [116] of the demons.[97] You will see their full power and various temptations. Indeed, it was for this reason that he wrote about these subjects, in order that those who read about them might be comforted knowing that they are not alone in suffering such temptations, and he showed us how such thoughts could be mastered through this or that kind of practice.[98] It is remarkable that such a person managed to escape notice from the beginning.

The Demons of Fornication Attacks Evagrius (LH 38.11)

22   One time the demons so increased in him the desire for fornication that he thought in his heart that God had abandoned him, as he told us, and he spent the whole night standing naked and praying in the cistern of water in winter until his flesh became as hard as rock.

The Spirit of Blasphemy Attacks Him (LH 38.11)

23   Another time, moreover, the spirit of blasphemy tormented him and he spent forty days without entering under the lintel of a cell until his whole body was covered with vermin like the body of an irrational animal [Dan 4:25–30].[99]

---

[97]Possibly, the *Praktikos.*

[98]This must be a reference to the *Antirrhetikos*; see Bunge, *Briefe*, 181.

[99]Palladius has several times emphasized Evagrius' reasoning and intellect (*kati*); here Evagrius is like an irrational (*atkati*) animal.

Evagrius' Mystical Ascent

24 *A few days later he told us about the revelations he had seen. He never hid anything*[100] *from his disciples.*[101] *"It happened," he said, "while I was sitting in my cell* [117] *at night with the lamp burning beside me, meditatively reading*[102] *one of the prophets. In the middle of the night I became enraptured and I found myself as though I were in a dream in sleep and I saw myself as though I were suspended in the air up to the clouds and I looked down on the whole inhabited world.*[103] *And the one who suspended me said to me, 'Do you see all these things?' He raised me up to the clouds and I saw the whole universe at the same time. I said to him, 'Yes.' He said to me, 'I am going to give you a commandment. If you keep it, you will be the ruler of all these things that you see.' He spoke to me again, 'Go, be compassionate, humble, and keep your thoughts pointed straight to God. You will rule over all these things.' When he had finished saying these things to me, I saw myself holding the book once again with the wick burning and I did not know how I had been taken up to the clouds. Whether I was in the flesh, I do not know; God knows. Or whether I was in the mind, once again I do not know"* [2 Cor 12:2]. *And so he contended with*[104] *these two virtues [of compassion and humility] as though he possessed all the virtues.*

[100]Adding *hli* with Vogüé.

[101]"He never hid anything from his disciples." This contradicts Evagrius' explicit teaching. For example: *Letter to Anatolius* 9 (i.e., the preface to the *Praktikos*): "Some things I have veiled and made obscure, to avoid giving what is holy to dogs and casting pearls before swine. But it will all be clear to those who have embarked on the same route"; *Gnostikos* 23: "It is necessary sometimes to feign ignorance, because those who are asking questions are not worthy to hear. And you will be telling the truth—since you are tied to a body and you do not now have an integrated knowledge of things." Evagrius seems in fact to have organized the *Kephalaia Gnostika* in such a way so as not to be too systematic, lest those who were not ready for the truth should have access to it.

[102]Coptic/Gk: -*meletan*; see n. 82 above.

[103]In the *Life of Antony* 65.2, one time when Antony was about to eat, "he stood up to pray close to the ninth hour when he perceived that he was being carried off in thought and, amazing to relate, stood there looking at himself as if he were outside himself and were being led into the air by certain beings."

[104]Coptic *ejen* is equally ambiguous, suggesting "for," "over," "on account of," and even "against."

Evagrius Teaches about Humility

25   He used to say that humility leads the intellect into right knowledge, drawing it upward, for it is written, [118] *"He shall teach the humble their paths"* [Ps 24:9].[105] *Indeed, this virtue is one the angels possess.* Concerning the purity of the body, he used to say that *"the monks are not alone with the virgins in possessing it. This virtue is theirs but it is also a virtue that numerous lay persons have who maintain purity, but since not all of them possess purity of body, 'seek out,' it says, 'peace with everyone, and purity, without which no one will see the Lord' "* [Heb 12:14].

The Purity of His Language

26   It was impossible to find a worldly word in the mouth of Apa Evagrius or a mocking word, and he refused to listen to another person using such words.

Evagrius Saves a Tribune's Wife in Palestine[106]

27   We also heard about this other wonderful matter: When[107] he fled from Apa Theophilus, who wanted to make him bishop of Thmoui,[108] he fled and went to Palestine and happened upon a tribune's wife who was possessed by an unclean demonic spirit. She would enjoy nothing from all of creation, for the demon taught her this practice as though this were the way the angels lived. Furthermore, she had not gone to her

---

[105]Ps 24:9 is an important verse for Evagrius [BV]. "Paths" translates *mōit* while "leads" translates *či mōit.*

[106]Evagrius' letters do not mention this event, which is fascinating for what it reveals both religiously and sociologically. If it took place, it was undoubtedly while he was on his way to see Rufinus and Melania.

[107]Reading *hoten* with Vogüé instead of *haten.*

[108]Thmuis. See par. 19 above.

husband's bed for many years. [119] *When Apa Evagrius the man of God*[109] *encountered her, he returned the woman's heart to God by means of a single word and a single prayer,*[110] *she and her husband at the same time. For she used to repeat some things said by philosophers outside of the faith without understanding what she was saying, saying things that would have been wonderful if another person had said them. Evagrius gained her salvation in the Lord and brought about her reconciliation*[111] *with her husband in peace.*

Discerning Good and Evil Events

28   *One time when he was in the desert, an old man who was fleeing from the presbyterate came to see him. While he was on his way, walking on the road, his bread gave out. When his disciple was about to faint from hunger, he stopped on the road and an angel placed a pair of loaves before him and put them on the road that led into*[112] *the mountain. When the old man arrived at Apa Evagrius', he said to him, "When I was on my way to see you, I and my servant, we got hungry on the road. We did not find bread to eat. My servant was about to collapse from not eating and after we placed some skins down on the ground, we genuflected. While we were bent to the ground, the smell of hot bread came to us and when I got up I found* [120] *two loaves of hot bread in front of me and when each of us had taken a loaf, we ate it, we recovered our strength, we started walking, and came to you." Indeed, I myself happened to be sitting there while he said these words to Apa Evagrius concerning the miracle that had happened to him. "Tell me, therefore," he said, "whether or not a demon has the power to do something like this."*[113]

---

[109]This epithet is applied to Antony in the *Life of Antony* 93.1.

[110]Adding *nem oueuchē nouōt* with Vogüé.

[111]Reading *hōtp* with Vogüé instead of *hōpt*.

[112]Adding *pimōit mmoshi hi* with Vogüé.

[113]Could the monk be thinking of Antony's experience (*Life of Antony* 40.3–4): "One day while I was fasting, the Deceiver came dressed like a monk. He had bread that was illusory and advised me, 'Eat, and stop all these sufferings. You are only

Apa Evagrius said to him, "You and I have both had such events happen to us. A few days ago I too went to visit the brothers. As I was walking along, I found on the road a money purse with three solidi in it. I stopped and sat down beside it lest someone had dropped it and would not be back to search for it.[114] *Although I spent a day sitting there, no one came to look for the money. I did not know where I could send the money because in truth I did not know who it belonged to. I sent [my steward] to the villages closest to me to ask whether or not someone*[115] *had lost a money purse the past few days. When I didn't find anyone, I ordered*[116] *my steward to distribute the money to strangers. Whether it was an angel or whether it was a demon that had left the purse, we distributed the money.*[117] *As for you and me, whether*[118] *what happened in our cases occurred on account of an angel or on account of a demon, let us give glory to God, for occurrences like these do not profit the soul at all except to purify it.*[119] *Nevertheless, I give glory to you*[120] *for having received* [121] *food from an angel. Yes, it is possible for demons to steal some loaves of bread and bring them to someone, but such loaves will not nourish the body because things that belong to demons stink*[121] *and if something comes from the demons the*

human and will grow weak.' But I recognized his deceitfulness and stood up to pray"?

[114] Add with Vogüé *ouoh etaiōsk eihemsi khatots je mēpōs ashei nsa ouai nteftasthof ntefkōti nsōs.* For a similar story, see *Life of Antony* 11–12.

[115] Reading *aouon* with Vogüé instead of *ouon.*

[116] Reading *tisharo* with Vogüé instead of *tisharos.*

[117] Reading *enichria* with Vogüé instead of *enichēra.*

[118] Reading *ite* with Vogüé instead of *pe.*

[119] For Evagrius, gold was not necessarily demonic; it was the passions that caused problems, not things in themselves. See Evagrius Ponticus *De diversis malgnis cogitationibus* 7 (PG 79.1208–1209), and *In Psalmos* 145.8, cited in Bunge, *Briefe,* 122.

[120] Now it is appropriate for Evagrius to give glory (*ti ōou*) because the monk has been glorified by God and the angels. See n. 30 above.

[121] A common belief among the monks. In *Life of Antony* 63.1–3, "Antony went down to the outer monastic cells and was asked to get on a boat and pray with the monks" where "he alone perceived a terrible and very acrid stench . . . a young man possessed by a demon (he had gotten on before them and hidden himself on the boat) suddenly cried out. Antony rebuked the demon in the name of our Lord Jesus Christ and it left the young man. The young man became well and everyone knew that the stench had come from the demon."

soul is confused when it sees it.[122] *If, however, it comes from the angels,
the soul is not confused but remains steadfast and at peace at that
time.*[123] *Therefore, the person who is worthy to receive food from the
angels first of all possesses discernment in thinking about the saying of
the Apostle, who says, 'Solid food is for the perfect, for those whose fac-
ulties have been trained by practice to distinguish evil from good' "*
[Heb 5:14].[124]

Evagrius' Encounter with Demons Disguised as Servants of the Church (LH 38.11)[125]

29   *Once again, three demons in the form of servants of the Church
came to see him one day in the heat of midday,*[126] *and they were dressed
in such a way that they were able to prevent him from recognizing them
and seeing that they were demons.*[127] *On account of this, after they had
left and he found the door closed, he realized that they were demons,
but he did not realize it at first.* [122] *They had given the appearance of*

[122]In the *Life of Antony* 35.4, Antony voices a similar sentiment: "A vision that
comes from the saints is not fraught with confusion."

[123]Such an understanding occurs commonly in Evagrius' writings [BV]. On the
wiles of the demons and ways of discerning them, see *Life of Antony* 21–43.

[124]According to Evagrius, food from angels is usually synonymous with knowledge [BV]. On discernment, see *Life of Antony* 22.3, 38.5, 44.1, 88.1–2, and Cassian *Conferences* 2.4.4.

[125]See *Ad monachos* 126 [BV]. Although this paragraph has a parallel in *LH* 38.11,
the version here is so much longer that I have italicized the entire paragraph. *LH* 38.11
reads like a condensation (Meyer, 113–14): "Three demons disguised as clerics attacked
him in broad daylight and they examined him as regards the faith; one said he was an
Arian, one a Eunomian, and the third said he was an Apollinarian. He got around
them with his knowledge and a few words." See the discussion in the General Introduction above and Appendix III for a parallel translation of the Greek and Coptic versions.

[126]These would therefore be the "noonday demons" of *acedia*: spiritual torpor
and boredom.

[127]In the *Life of Antony* 25.3, Antony says, "In addition, changing themselves into
the forms of monks, [the demons] pretend to speak like the faithful in order to lead
them astray with this seeming likeness, and afterwards, they drag away those who
have been deceived by them wherever they wish."

discussing with him the subject of faith in the Scriptures, and each of
them told him his concern and they said to him, "We have heard it said
about you that you speak articulately about the orthodox faith; there-
fore, we have come to you so you might satisfy our concerns." He said
to them, "Ask what you wish."

The first said to him, "I am a Eunomian.[128] *I have come to you so*
you might tell me whether the Father is begotten or unbegotten."[129]
Apa Evagrius said to him, "I will not answer you because you have
asked a bad question, for it is not right to talk about the nature of the
Unbegotten and to inquire whether it is begotten or unbegotten."[130]

When the first realized that Evagrius had defeated him, he pushed
his companion forward. When he had come forward, he first said [to
his companion], "You've put your question badly." Apa Evagrius said
to him, "And you, who are you?" He said, "I am an Arian." Apa Eva-
grius said to him, "And you in turn, what do you seek?" He said to him,
"I am asking about the Holy Spirit and about the body of Christ,
whether or not it was truly him whom Mary bore."[131] *Saint Evagrius*
said to him, [123] *"The Holy Spirit is neither an offspring*[132] *nor a crea-*
ture. All creatures are limited to a place. All creatures are subject to
change and are sanctified by him who is better than they."[133]

[The third one said,] "You have defeated these two, for some [. . .]
will you wish to speak to me too?"[134] *The old man said to [him], "What*
do you seek, you, you who pride yourself in doing battle?"[135] *The*
demon said to him, "Me? I'm not arguing with anyone, but my mind

[128]According to the Gk (Cotelier 117,17; see Appendix III); Coptic *eumenios*.

[129]Coptic uses the technical Gk vocabulary *gennētos* and *agennētos*.

[130]Here the Coptic equivalents of *mise* and *athmise* are used. This response is true
to Evagrius' thinking; see Evagrius, *Gnostikos* 27 and 41; A. Guillaumont, ed., *Évagre
le Pontique: Le Gnostique ou à celui qui est devenu digne de la science* (SC 356; Paris:
Cerf, 1989), 132–33, 166–67. See the discussion in the Introduction to this volume.

[131]"Bore," *mas-*, is etymologically related to *mise*, "begotten."

[132]Coptic *-mise*; see the previous two notes.

[133]See *Life of Antony* 69 for Antony's refutation of Arianism.

[134]The manuscript is damaged here and elsewhere at the end. BV suggest, based
on *LH* 38.11, that the third demon is an Apollinarian.

[135]See *Life of Antony* 77–85.

is not persuaded or certain that Christ received human intelligence. Rather, in place of intellect God himself was in him. Indeed, it is impossible for human intelligence to cast out the Prince of Demons from human beings and defeat him. Indeed, human intelligence can not exist in the body with God."

Apa Evagrius said to him, "If he did not receive human intelligence, he did not receive human flesh either. If,[136] therefore, [he] received human flesh from [Mary the] holy Virgin, then [he] also [became] human, with a soul [and intellect], being complete in everything human except sin alone [Heb 4:15]. For it is impossible for the body to exist [124] [without receiving] a soul and intellect. If, therefore, he did not receive these, then he is called Christ in vain. Therefore, the unchangeable Logos, the only-begotten Son of the Father [Jn 1:14, 3:18], received a human body and soul and intellect and everything human except sin.

"Therefore let it suffice us at present to offer solely the apostle Paul as a witness, who, bringing together the faith in a single unity,[137] speaks of a single divinity and a single royalty: the consubstantial and unchanging Trinity. 'For,' he says, 'one is God, one is the mediator between God and humankind, Jesus Christ,'[138] the Son of God the Father, with the one Holy Spirit, one baptism,[139] one Catholic Church, one resurrection of the dead at the time of [. . .] as [Paul has said][140] [. . .] you (pl.) deny the full mystery of the Holy Trinity.[141] One of you has made the Logos a creature, another has made the Holy Spirit a creature and [denied] the body of Christ, and another has killed the soul and body of Christ [. . .][142]

[136]Reading *isje* with BV instead of *ie je.*

[137]*Monas,* the Monad of Greek philosophical thought, taken over by Christian theologians in order to speak of the Trinity.

[138]See 1 Tim 2:5. Both "single" and "one" translate Coptic *ouōt.*

[139]Adding *ouōms nouōt* with Vogüé.

[140]This is conjectural; BV suggest, on the basis of the Greek, "as I see." Note the creedal character of Evagrius' words.

[141]See *Ad monachos* 134.

[142]The manuscript breaks off here. See Appendix III for the Gk conclusion of this story.

CHAPTER THREE

The Life of Macarius the Great
(*Lausiac History* 17)

Introduction

The Life of Macarius the Great[1]

There are two recensions of the Coptic *Life of Macarius the Great*, which should be distinguished from the later *Life of Macarius of Scetis* attributed to Sarapion of Thmuis (translated in chapter 3 of *Saint Macarius the Spiritbearer*). The Long Recension of the *Life* replicates most of *Lausiac History* 17, with some additional material, most notably par. 6 on the follower of Hieracas (see below for a brief discussion of it), while the Short Recension has only five of the thirteen paragraphs of Palladius' *History* (*LH* 17.6–9, 11).[2] Except for one slightly displaced paragraph (8 = *LH* 17.10), the twelve paragraphs of the Coptic *Life* follow the order of chapter 17 of the *Lausiac History*. The Coptic *Life* then has three additional paragraphs: par. 10, Abba Macarius and Abba Amoun; par. 11, the mighty deeds and works of Abba Macarius; and, most interesting, par. 12, the death of Abba Macarius.

Palladius includes only one sentence about Macarius' death (17.13): "I did not meet him, since he had fallen asleep a year before

[1]For information on Macarius the Great, see the Introduction to the companion volume to this one, *Saint Macarius the Spiritbearer*.

[2]The Short Recension is clearly a translation of *LH* 17:6–9 and part of 17.11.

I entered the desert." The Coptic *Life*, by contrast, narrates at some length Macarius' ascent to heaven and reception on high. Par. 12 of the Coptic *Life*, thus, is classic hagiography: an editor, dissatisfied with the lack of an edifying conclusion to Macarius' life (his holy death), appended the story of the saint's assumption into heaven. He does, however, vouch for the story by giving his source—"Abba Paphnutius, the disciple of Abba Macarius." The *Life of Macarius of Scetis* 36 agrees that the "holy man Abba Paphnutius, who was the greatest of the saint's disciples ... assumed the fatherhood in the holy places after Abba Macarius." The problem here is that *Lausiac History* 18.27, devoted to the life of Macarius of Alexandria (= Coptic *Life of Macarius of Alexandria* 18 in the present volume), says that Paphnutius was a disciple of the Alexandrian. Paphnutius (the Latinized form of Papnoute) was a common Coptic name, so it is possible that each Macarius had a disciple named Paphnutius. Palladius speaks of "Paphnutius of Scetis" (*LH* 46.2) and Cassian locates Paphnutius in Scetis (*Conferences* 3.1.1, 10.3.1, 18.15.1), where Macarius lived, which would seem to indicate that this Paphnutius was indeed the disciple of Macarius the Great. But Cassian does not connect Paphnutius with Macarius the Great; Paphnutius was a priest, and he was already an old man at the time that Cassian and Palladius visited the desert. Thus, this Paphnutius can not have been a disciple of Macarius the Great. Given the confusion in antiquity between the two Macarii,[3] it seems possible that the editor who appended the hagiographical ending to the *Life of Macarius the Great*, or his source, mixed up the two Macarii and so gave the disciple of Macarius of Alexandria to Macarius of Egypt, but this is not certain.[4]

[3]See Antoine Guillaumont, "Le problème des deux Macaires" and Gabriel Bunge, "Évagre le Pontique et les deux Macaires." As Guillaumont, 48, aptly calls it: "le désaccord profond entre ceux qui paraissent être les premiers témoins." For one example in the texts published here: the *Life of Macarius of Alexandria* 7 offers a story about Macarius' visit to the Pachomians at Tabennesi, a visit seemingly confirmed by *AP* Macarius of Alexandria 2; however, the *Sayings of Macarius of Egypt* 26 (found in *Saint Macarius the Spiritbearer*) seems to give a much shorter version of this story, attributing it to Macarius the Great.

[4]Either he was followed in this attribution by the *Life of Macarius of Scetis* or each

One must caution, however, that this editor is not necessarily the same person responsible for the beginning of the rather intriguing *Life* (words in italics are not found in the *Lausiac History*):

> I will first tell about the Egyptian; *he finished life in the body first, before the Alexandrian, and it was also he who buried the body of Abba Antony.* He spent sixty-five years living in the desert and died in his ninety-seventh year. *Two years after his leaving the body, I entered the monastic community* and met the Alexandrian, *who lived another two years.*[5] *When I encountered the true disciples of the Egyptian I implored them and they told me about a few of his virtues and ascetic practices. Abba Evagrius was also very close to him; he himself told me about a few of his virtues too.*

In *Lausiac History* 17.13 Palladius says that Macarius fell asleep a year before he came to the desert; here it is two years. The author of the Coptic *Life* goes on to add that Macarius of Alexandria lived another two years, which is a reasonable statement.[6] This author hurts his historical credibility, however, by saying that Macarius of Egypt had buried Antony; in this he is followed by the *Life of Macarius of Scetis* 19. The hagiographical intention of the latter is to make Macarius the disciple of Antony the Great, a tradition followed by the *Historia monachorum* 28.1 when it says that Macarius was "the disciple of Antony." It was widely reported in antiquity that *a* Macarius had interred the great Antony.[7] Given the close association between

Macarius did have a disciple named Paphnutius. The *Sayings, Virtues,* and *Life of Macarius of Scetis* all say he had a disciple named Paphnutius; for these works, see *Saint Macarius the Spiritbearer.*

[5]This would be about 392.

[6]In *LH* 18.1 Palladius says that Macarius of Alexandria was alive for three years. The *Historia monachorum* 23.1, an account of a trip made in 394–95, says that Macarius "had just died." Guillaumont, "Le problème," 46, dates the death of Macarius of Alexandria to 394.

[7]In the *Life of Antony* 91, Antony commands two—unnamed—disciples to bury him, and in par. 92 they do so. Jerome, *Life of Paul* 1, gives these two disciples names:

Macarius the Great and Antony (see *AP* Macarius 4 and 26), it is not surprising that the Macarius who buried Antony (according to Jerome and Palladius) became Macarius the Great. Since Palladius clearly states (*LH* 21.1), however, that Antony's Macarius still dwelt in Pispir, Antony's outer mountain, he can not have also believed that Macarius the Great buried Antony.[8] It is clear that later monastic tradition, in its desire to associate *more closely* two of the great founders of monasticism (an association, as noted above, that does have historical basis) and create a monastic genealogy connecting Antony with Macarius, conflated Macarius of Pispir and Macarius of Scetis.[9]

The chronology is close, but the mistaken statement that Macarius the Great buried Antony is wrong. Could it be an editorial (or scribal) gloss—that is, something not written originally by Palladius? This seems possible because of what the author goes on to say: that he learned about Macarius directly from the saint's disciples—and from Evagrius. In the *Virtues of Macarius*, Evagrius "the sage" is the interlocutor of Macarius most often mentioned. That such a statement about Evagrius could come from Palladius is not only plausible but likely. In fact, the author of the Coptic *Life* is careful to indicate his sources (pars. 4, 6, 10, 12; all but the last do not have parallels in the *LH*). The fact that the author gives Evagrius as a prominent source, and that this fact does not appear in the *Lausiac History*,

Macarius and Amatus, but it is the latter who buries Antony. Jerome, however, does not connect this Macarius with Macarius of Egypt. *LH* 21.1 gives these same names and says the two buried Antony.

[8] In *LH* 21.1 Cronius, the narrator of the information about "Macarius," does not connect Macarius of Pispir with Macarius the Great; more importantly, in *LH* 17, Palladius does not connect Macarius the Great with Antony's burial, something he surely would have done had he known the connection.

[9] Chronology also argues against identifying Macarius of Scetis with Macarius of Pispir: Macarius was in Scetis by 330 and Antony died in 356, so Macarius the Great could not have been a disciple of Antony, living in Pispir, when Antony died. The Coptic *Life of Macarius of Scetis* solves this problem by having Macarius journey to Pispir just in time for Antony's death, but the other early monastic sources indicate that Antony was buried by two disciples. These two, presumably, would have been living with him for a while.

makes it seem credible that this source was edited out later, either by an editor or by Palladius himself. (On the expunging of Evagrius from the monastic record, see the General Introduction to this volume.) If, therefore, the Coptic *Life* represents an early draft by Palladius of what would become the *Lausiac History*, Palladius himself could have deleted parts of it later. Or, if the Coptic *Life* represents an unexpurgated version of the *Lausiac History*, the extra material found in the Coptic *Life* could have been effaced in the Greek tradition by a redactor. In any case, there is at least a possibility that *some* of the extra material in the Coptic *Life* is Palladian. I suggest that the statements about Evagrius do go back to Palladius, and that some of the other Coptic material was added during later transmission by scribes and editors.

Undoubtedly the most important of this extra material is par. 6, on the monk led astray by an evil spirit that "wrapped him in the erroneous doctrine of heresies that are named after Hieracas."[10] The account of the follower of Hieracas preserved in *Lausiac History* 17.11 is obviously an epitome, combined (badly) with the story of a demoniac. The Coptic *Life* preserves what must have been the original, longer, version (par. 5) and follows it with the story of the demoniac (par. 6). We know from other sources that Hieracas lived in a monastery outside Leontopolis, a city in the southern delta. He flourished about 335 and died before 370;[11] therefore this account of a run-in between one of his followers and Macarius is at least chronologically accurate and probably took place in some form. According to the Coptic *Life*, Hieracas' heretical doctrines were many; he held that

> our Lord Jesus Christ did not assume human flesh but a
> heavenly flesh that he brought when he came to earth. They

[10]The monk is later called "Hieracas" in the story, but this is a mistake.

[11]David Brakke, *Athanasius and the Politics of Asceticism* (Oxford: Clarendon, 1995), 45. Brakke discusses Athanasius' confrontations with Hieracas on pages 44–57. See also the discussion by James Goehring, *Ascetics, Society, and the Desert*, 110–33.

say that there is no resurrection of the flesh for human beings. They also say that there are three principles, God, Matter, and Evil, and on account of this they dare to say with certainty that the Logos of God did not descend into humanity nor did he become completely human in everything human except sin alone. They say that the Logos of God was not the cause of creation.They say that through free will all human beings choose for themselves evil and thinking and acting like animals.

But in order not to proceed with a multitude of words about this heresy, let me simply say that that man led a multitude of souls astray: he led astray five hundred souls, both men and women. Indeed, he rejected marriage, saying that no man marrying a woman would enter the kingdom of God.

The account given here of Hieracas' thought is reasonably accurate.[12] The assertion that the Hieracites stressed free will is at odds with Athanasius' polemic against their leader.[13] Presumably the encounter between Macarius and the disciple of Hieracas took place after Hieracas' death; if so, this account is important because it shows the lingering influence of Hieracas and the felt need of the orthodox monks to combat it, probably sometime in the second half

[12]See Brakke, *Athanasius,* for a full discussion. The most complete ancient source on Hieracas is Epiphanius *Panarion* 67 (PG 42.172–84). See also Sozomen *EH* 3.14. Augustine *De haeresibus* 47 (PL 42.38–39), gives this summary: "The Hieracites, whose founder is called Hieraca, deny the resurrection of the body. They receive only monks, nuns, and the unmarried into communion with them. They say that children do not belong to the kingdom of heaven, for they have gained no merit by struggling against sin"; See Liguori G. Müller, *The De Haeresibus of Saint Augustine* (Washington, D.C.: The Catholic University of America Press, 1956), 96 (Latin), 97 (English). For modern assessments, see G. Bareille, "Hiéracas," *Dictionnaire de spiritualité catholique* 6.2359–61; J. Kraus, "Hierakas," *Lexikon für Theologie und Kirche* (2nd ed.; Freiburg, 1957–), 5.321; Karl Heussi, *Der Ursprung des Mönchtums* (Tübingen, 1936), 58–65; Bernhard Lohse, *Askese und Mönchtum in der Antike und in der alten Kirche* (Munich, 1969), 179–81, and Goehring, *Ascetics, Society, and the Desert.*

[13]See Brakke, *Athanasius,* 49–51.

of the fourth century. As David Brakke has concluded, Hieracas' beliefs were "at home in the loosely related Christian groups of the third century, but increasingly out of place in the developing imperial Church of the fourth. Certainly the social practices of Hieracas and his followers did not cohere with the institutional, episcopally centered Christianity that Athanasius was forming."[14] It is striking that the anti-heresiological concerns of the author of the Coptic *Life of Macarius* are with Hieracas' theology and not with his ascetical teachings and the resulting social practices which so vexed Athanasius. Presumably these practices would have also challenged Macarius and his followers; perhaps this unnamed follower of Hieracas was a lone figure and the Hieracite communities had now vanished and thus were no longer a threat.

As the account of the disciple of Hieracas shows, the *Life* is of more than passing interest, both in its parts and as a whole; in conclusion, therefore, it is worth quoting in full one scholar's appreciation of it:

One must recognize that the talent of the redactor, in these passages, is not slight, his information is not of the usual kind, and his account contains everything one would wish from an historian. Called on to reveal facts that smack of the marvelous, he works hard to specify the sources he has drawn on, as he does to be exact about the dates of the events he is narrating, according to the needs of the narration. Thus he informs us, at the beginning, that it was the second year after the death of Macarius of Egypt that he arrived at the Mountain, two years before the death of Macarius of Alexandria. He also questioned the very disciples of the great monk, and he sought information in particular from one of them whose name he gives us: Evagrius. And gradually, as he tells his story, he takes care to distinguish what he has seen from what he has heard told. He always seems to have present in

[14]Brakke, *Athanasius*, 48.

his mind what he wrote at the outset, alluding to his verac-
ity. Laying stress on precise documentation, full of details,
the story in our text, said to be exaggerated, appears nevertheless in a more lively form, with a more revealing personality, than that which we have in the brief account [that is,
the short recension discussed above]. Our author, more
often than the latter, puts himself in the action. More often
he addresses the reader, whom he connects to his narration,
either by challenging him in the course of his account or by
making him participate in what he narrates. He lets the persons he treats live and move; he lets them speak. He is fond
of a direct style in preference to a simple telling of their
words or feelings. He puts himself in the action up to seven
times. Overall he maintains a tone that disparages nothing,
a sense of discretion that falsifies nothing, and everywhere
he demonstrates moderation without ever deviating into
any kind of excess, without spilling over into prolixity or
obscurity. One does not see anything one could cut out of his
story, nor what could be considered useless or irrelevant. If
he is only a redactor, he incontestably evinces an uncommon
mastery in his art, and one can not deny a talent in him at
least equal to the original. It seems that, moreover, just as
when one has read the brief text one has the impression of
confronting an abridgment, a summary, likewise when one
has read our redactor, the brief text does not strike one as
having served him as a rough draft.[15]

The Coptic *Life of Macarius the Great* was read in the Coptic
Synaxary on 27 Phamenot.

[15]M. Chaîne, "La double recension de l'*Histoire Lausique* dans la version copte,"
Revue de l'orient chrétien, 25 (1925–26): 232–75, at 236–37.

SYNOPTIC TABLE

The Coptic *Life of Macarius & Lausiac History 17*

Coptic *Life*	Lausiac History
The Long Recension	
1. Prologue	*LH* 17.1
2. Abba Macarius the Egyptian	*LH* 17.2
3. Macarius Foresees the Ruin of His Disciple John	*LH* 17.3–4
4. His Way of Life and Virtues and Ascetic Practices	*LH* 17.5
5. Abba Macarius Saves a Woman Changed into a Mare	*LH* 17.6–9
6. Concerning a Follower of Hieracas	*LH* 17.11
7. Abba Macarius Heals a Young Man	*LH* 17.11
8. Macarius' Secret Tunnel	*LH* 17.10
9. Macarius Rebukes the Widow for her Lack of Charity	*LH* 17.12–13
10. Abba Macarius and Abba Amoun	—
11. The Mighty Deeds and Virtues of Abba Macarius	—
12. The Death of Abba Macarius	—
The Short Recension	
1. Abba Macarius Saves a Woman Changed into a Mare	*LH* 17.6–9
2. Abba Macarius Heals a Young Man	*LH* 17.11

CONCERNING ABBA MACARIUS THE GREAT[16]

[THE LONG RECENSION]

Prologue (LH 17.1)[17]

1   [239] It is necessary now for us to speak about the works first of
Abba Macarius the Egyptian and then of Abba Macarius the Alexandrian, *for the two of them were great on account of their way of life and
ascetic practice and were* famous *throughout the whole monastic
world*[18] *on account of their labors.* Those who hear about them, if
they are unbelieving, will not believe that such men existed or did
the things they did.[19] Therefore I hesitate to write about them, so
many are their deeds and so difficult to believe, lest some think me
a liar, for truly it is written, "The Lord will destroy everyone who tells
lies" [Ps 5:6].[20] You yourself know, since you are a believer, that I do
not speak lies, *for you have devoted yourself to numerous ascetic practices.*[21] Therefore, do not disbelieve their histories. With regard to
these two Macarii, then, one was an Egyptian while the other was an
Alexandrian and early in life a vendor of confectionaries.[22]

[16]Translated from M. Chaîne, "La double recension," 239–59, with additional textual material supplied by Adalbert de Vogüé, "La version copte du chapitre XVII de
l'Histoire Lausiaque: Les deux éditeurs et les trois manuscrits," *Orientalia* 58.4 (1989):
510–24. Numbers in brackets give the pagination of Chaîne's text. Abbreviations: **a** =
Vat. Copt 59, **b** = Vat. Copt 62, **c** = Vat. Copt 64. Title: **b**: the Egyptian; **c** + and Abba
Macarius the Alexandrian.

[17]Section titles and paragraphing are my own. Portions in italics are lacking in
Gk. Paragraphs without "*LH*" in parentheses lack parallels with the *Lausiac History*.
Paragraph numbers do not correspond to *LH* but are given for ease of reference.

[18]Perhaps "all of monastic Egypt," literally "all of monasticism."

[19]See *Life of Antony* Prologue.

[20]Gk adds: "as the Holy Spirit declared."

[21]See *Life of Antony* Prologue.

[22]Coptic -*trakēmata* (**ac**: -*dragēmata*) = Gk *tragēmata* (LSJ 1809A), dried fruits
or sweetmeats, confectionary, sold as dessert. Note the distinction between Alexandria and the rest of Egypt.

Abba Macarius the Egyptian (LH 17.2)

2   I will first tell about the Egyptian; *he finished life in the body first, before the Alexandrian, and it was also he who buried the body of Abba Antony.*[23] He spent sixty-five years living [240] in the desert and died in his ninety-seventh year.[24] *Two years after his leaving the body, I entered the monastic settlement*[25] and met the Alexandrian,[26] *who lived another two years.*[27] *When I encountered the true disciples of the Egyptian I implored them to tell me about him and they informed me about a few of his virtues and ascetic practices. Abba Evagrius was also very close to him;*[28] *he himself told me about a few of his virtues too.* They told me that from the time he was little he was considered worthy to have received great discernment; his counsel was so discerning that he was called "the old man" from his youth.[29] On account of his knowledge,[30] therefore, which was pure, he made great progress. When he was forty years old he was worthy to receive grace against spirits; *he healed every kind of human illness* and also received the grace of prophecy:[31] *often he told those who had faith in his words about events that had not yet happened, and they happened.*

[23]In the *Life of Antony* 91, Antony commands two (unnamed) disciples to bury him, and in par. 92 they do so. Jerome, *Life of Paul* 1, gives these two disciples names: Macarius and Amatus, but it is the latter who buries Antony. *LH* 21.1 gives these same names and says the two buried Antony. The *Historia Monachorum* 21.1 and *Life of Macarius of Scetis* 19 say that Macarius of Egypt was a disciple of Antony.

[24]*LH*: ninety years, with which Sozomen *EH* 3.14, concurs, adding that Macarius spent sixty years in the desert.

[25]Or "mountain," Coptic *pitōou*.

[26]See *LH* 18.1 where Palladius says he met "the other Macarius, . . . the one from Alexandria."

[27]This would be about 392. In *LH* 18.1 Palladius says that Macarius of Alexandria was alive for three years.

[28]This important sentence, lacking in the *LH*, may also suggest discipleship on Evagrius' part (*nafkeh erof*; Crum 133A). BV translate as "Évagre . . . était très lié avec lui," and Chaîne "Évagrius . . . qui était son grand émule."

[29]Gk: *paidariogeronta.*

[30]His knowledge: Gk, "this." "Knowledge," *kati*, is also an important virtue in the *Life of Evagrius*.

[31]Gk +: He was even deemed worthy of the priesthood.

Macarius Foresees the Ruin of His Disciple John (LH 17.3–4)

3   Two disciples lived *alone* with him in the interior of the *great* desert called Scetis. One of his disciples, on account of the sick who came to Abba Macarius, lived near him in order to serve them, while the other lived *alone* in an *enclosed*[32] cell in the great interior desert.[33] When a little time had passed, Abba Macarius, with enlightened fore-sight,[34] began to see what would happen to his disciple, and he said to him,[35] "John, *my servant*, listen to me, my child, and receive my instruction, for truly you are being tempted *by a passion and at pres-ent you do not know it. Indeed, I see that* [241] the spirit of avarice is about to master[36] you and I know that if you listen to me you will fin-ish your life[37] in this dwelling and will be honored by all and[38] 'the scourge will not touch your dwelling' [Ps 91:10]. But if you do not lis-ten to me, your end will be ugly, like that of Gehazi, *the servant of Elisha,* for truly you are sick with his passion" [2 Kg 5:20–27].[39]

It turned out therefore that when John did not listen to Saint[40] Abba Macarius, after the death of Abba Macarius, fifteen or twenty years later, he contracted leprosy[41] *over his whole body* so that you could not find the smallest place on his body where you could poke your finger [without its being contaminated],[42] for truly he was in the habit of stealing[43] money that was given to him to distribute to

[32]Coptic *orf* suggests a number of meanings here: apart, enclosed, quiet.

[33]In the great interior desert: Gk, "in a cell near by."

[34]Literally: "with the eye of light of his understanding" (*kati*).

[35]Gk +: "who later became a priest in his own place."

[36]In Coptic, the word for "to master, rule," *erčois*, uses the abbreviation *čs*, "Lord," that is used for Christ (cf. English "to lord it over someone"). Gk: tempting.

[37]Coptic *jōk ebol* suggests "perfect" (verb), which the Gk has.

[38]c + *ouoh.*

[39]Gehazi's passion (*pathos*) was to deceitfully obtain money from Naaman and then lie about it to Elisha. His "ugly" end was to be cursed with leprosy; see the next par.

[40]b: *piagos*; ac: *piagios.*

[41]b: *-kephalos*; c: *-kelaphos* (= Gk *kelephos*).

[42]This phrase, supplied from Gk, seems required for the sense, and may have been omitted accidentally.

[43]b: *ne shafkōlp*; c: *nafkōlp.*

the poor. This then was the prophecy of Saint Abba Macarius, *for he saw what would happen before it happened.*

His Way of Life and Virtues and Ascetic Practices (LH 17.5)

4　*With regard to his way of life, we will report it just as we heard. The first of his virtues was that he lived alone in the desert at all times. The Egyptians, to be sure, take great pride*[44] *in this ability, along with manual labor, which for them is a thing of beauty, along with poor quality food eaten in poverty and keeping vigil where you live while working with your hands.* But it is unnecessary to speak further about this old man's food and drink, for truly even those who neglect their ascetic practice do not find sufficient bread and water in the desert of Scetis,[45] either because of the poverty where they live or on account of zeal that leads each of them to asceticism.[46] *Truly that desert leads each person into feats* [242] *of asceticism, whether he wants to or not.* And concerning the great asceticism of the old man, they say about him that in everything that he undertook he turned his thoughts to union with God in everything he did so that when he prayed his thoughts would often fly to the heights and he would speak with God while abiding in the vision of heaven. And everyone was amazed at all the graces that God gave to him, and in all these things no one was able to surpass him in all the virtues or be greater than he.[47] God did[48] great miracles through this Abba Macarius the Egyptian, healings of those who were sick, all of which I will recount together, for he used to cast out numerous demons.[49]

[44]a omits; perhaps a scribe thought the word smacked too much of boastfulness.

[45]Do not find sufficient bread and water in the desert of Scetis: Gk, "one cannot find gluttony or indifference."

[46]See *Life of Antony* 7.6–7. See also Philo *De vita contemplativa* 34–35, reproduced by Eusebius *EH* 2.17.16–17 [BV].

[47]See *Life of Macarius of Scetis* 38 in *Saint Macarius the Spiritbearer.*

[48]Literally: "created."

[49]And concerning . . . demons: Gk, "And now I will speak of the rest of his asceticism, for he was said to be in continual ecstasy. He occupied himself much more with God than with earthly things, and these are the wonders told of him:".

Abba Macarius Saves a Woman Changed into a Mare (LH 17.6–9)[50]

5   An Egyptian fell in love with a free woman[51] who was married.[52] He had a word with her but she did not listen to him. When he saw that she would not give herself to him, he went to a magician's place and made this request, saying, "*I'm in love with a woman but she won't give herself to me.* Either force her to love me or stir up enmity between her and her husband so he will repudiate her *and I can take her as my wife.*"

When the magician had received a great deal of money from the Egyptian, he worked his wicked sorcerer's craft and cast a spell[53] over human eyes that caused them to see her as a mare.[54] *(It is not possible for a person to change God's creatures; only God can do so: he who*[55] *created them is the one who has the power to change the nature of his creatures as he wishes.)*[56] *Her husband spent many days with his clothes torn, mourning for his wife,* [243] *seeing her as a mare, and she spent many days without eating anything. If he gave her a bunch of hay, she would not eat it; if he gave her bread, she would not eat it.*[57] Her husband was amazed, saying, "How has my wife, who is lying in my bed, become a mare?" He would speak to her, weeping, but she gave him no reply.

He went and implored the priests of the Church, saying, "Come to my house and see the suffering that afflicts me." When they

[50]For a condensed version of this story with considerable differences, see *Historia Monachorum* 21.17 (Russell, trans., 110 and 151). See also the Short Recension below.

[51]Coptic *ouremhē nshimi*; Gk *eleutheras gunaikos* (Bartelink, ed., *La storia lausiaca*, 72). *Eleuthera* may designate a married woman, a widow, or a freedwoman.

[52]Gk +: "of good position." In both the Greek and Latin versions of this story in *Historia Monachorum*, told about Macarius the Great, the girl is not married but is a consecrated virgin and her parents, not her husband, take her to Abba Macarius.

[53]Literally: darkness.

[54]Gk simply says that he "caused her to assume the shape of a brood mare." See the next sentence.

[55]b: *phti*, God; ac: *phē*.

[56]This theological reflection is put into the mouth of Abba Macarius below.

[57]BV accidentally omit the second half of this sentence.

entered his house they saw her but did not understand what was taking place. When she came to her third day of not eating (she had eaten neither bread nor hay for two days), he said, "If I let her go on like this, she will die from starvation. I will rise and take her to the house of Abba Macarius, the man of God, so he will see her and know what is going on."[58] This happened so that the power of God that resided with Abba Macarius the Great might be manifested.

Her husband got up and put a bridle on her like a mare and led her to the desert *and brought her to Abba Macarius'*. When he arrived at the place, the brothers gathered together outside the church of Abba Macarius.[59] The brothers quarreled with the man, saying, *"Why have you dared to bring this female mare*[60] *up here to this monastic community? You have committed a very great sin.* Why then have you brought this female mare here with you?"

He said to them, "I have brought her *to the saint* so pity might be taken on her."

They said to him, "What's wrong with her?"

He said to them, "This is my wife and I do not know how she became a mare. Look, she hasn't eaten for three days."

They *left and* told the old man, [244] *saying, "There's a man outside over there in possession of* [61] *a mare and he's saying 'This is my wife and I do not know how she became a mare through magic.'"*[62] *What*

---

[58]Gk: At last, so that God might be praised and the virtue of the holy Macarius be made manifest, it entered into the mind of the husband to lead her out into the desert.

[59]Gk: by the cell of Abba Macarius; see n. 125 below. BV suggest, 107 n. 18, that perhaps the Coptic editor misread "church" (*ekklēsia*) for "cell" (*kellēs*), although the short recension (below) also reads "church."

[60]BV point out, 107 n. 19, that this redundancy (omitted by Chaîne in his translation) emphasizes that female animals were not allowed in the community, the same situation that exists today (with the exception of hens) on Mt Athos. See *Life of Macarius of Scetis* 32 for a similar situation. In Coptic, "female," *shimi*, is the same word as "wife."

[61]There may be a sly play on words here in Coptic. *Amoni* is a homonym meaning "to be in possession of" and "to pasture, feed."

[62]Note the repetition of oral literature—and how someone has slipped and added "through magic."

had God already told Abba Macarius concerning her? For they found him praying for her. Saint Abba Macarius *opened the door, came out, and saw her; he* said to the brothers, "It is you, rather, who are horses, you who have the eyes of horses. She is not a mare; rather you see her looking like a mare, for this is a woman and I am looking at her. *It is not possible for a person to change one of God's creatures into something else; rather, it is a spell[63] that has been placed over our human eyes. So you will know that this is the case, bring me that water over there."*

When they brought him the water, he prayed with the brothers, made the sign of the cross over it, blessed it, and sprinkled it over her head.[64] This immediately caused her to appear in the form of a woman, *speaking and giving thanks to God and to the old man in front of everyone.* And Abba Macarius *took some bread, blessed it,* gave it to her, and had her eat [Mt 14:20], *and she recovered her strength and everyone saw her become a woman. And he gave her this order: "Do not eat flesh lest the demon find the pleasure of flesh in you and return once again to you by means of the pleasure of heat and fleshly matter."* And he gave this order to her in these words: "Do not skip receiving the eucharist *a single Saturday, ever.[65]* Go to church regularly, *morning and evening, every day.* Because what has occurred happened because you went five weeks without partaking of the mysteries[66] *of Christ."* He dismissed her and she went home with her husband, *the two of them together* giving thanks to God.

Concerning a Follower of Hieracas (LH 17.11)[67]

6   [245] *I also heard from some trustworthy men about this other small matter concerning him. It happened that there was a monk, a*

[63]Literally: "darkness"; see above. Chaîne corrects *alol* to *hlol.*

[64]c: caused it to be sprinkled. Gk: "poured it on her bare skin from the head downward."

[65]*Sabbaton*; see Lampe 1220A(B). Chaîne translates "Sunday."

[66]Or: sacraments, *-mustērion* (pl).

[67]This section title is in the mss. b: *ethbe piaraka*; c: *ethbe pieraka.* This story is

man who lived in the deserts of the village of Boushēm,[68] *practicing
asceticism for many years with great and strenuous practices in the
great seclusion of the Great Desert, walking in purity of life, and he did
not ever pay a visit to an old man, for he was vain and full of himself.
After a while, the passion within him led him astray. A spirit of div-
ination,*[69] *that is, the demon of falsehood, came to dwell in him so that
he would tell people about numerous events that were going to happen
to them: he would say "they will happen," and they happened, and he
spoke about the waters of the Nile and about many other worldly
events that he learned about from the spirits.*[70] *As a result, he became
vain and his understanding of God was very clouded.*

*When the spirit knew that this man's heart was joined to him, he
first of all led him away from the orthodox faith and wrapped him in
the erroneous*[71] *doctrine of heresies that are named after Hieracas,*

summarized in one sentence in the *LH* (Meyer, 57): "A report went about concerning
him that he had brought a dead person to life to convince a heretic who did not
believe in the resurrection of the body." Therefore I have italicized this whole section.
The story occurs elsewhere: PG 34.209–16; *Historia Monachorum* 28.4 (Latin; Russell,
trans., 152); Cassian *Conference* 15.3 (where the unnamed heretic is a Eunomian; see
the Coptic *Life of Evagrius* 29); *AP* [1]490B (K 300), where the unnamed monk lived
near Arsinoë (Lucien Regnault, *Les Sentences des pères du désert: série des anonymes*
[Solesmes: Bellefontaine, 1985], 174–77). BV, 108 n. 25, mistakenly refer to *AP* 1490A
(Macarius S1). Evelyn White, 1.124–26, published two small Bohairic Coptic fragments found at the Monastery of Saint Macarius. See Appendix II for a similar story
about a certain Stephen. Toda Satoshi, "La Vie de S. Macaire l'Égyptien: État de la
question," *Analecta Bollandiana*, 118:3–4 (2000): 267–90, points out, 269, that Amélineau omitted the account of Hieracas from his text of the Coptic *Life of Macarius of
Scetis*, but that the story is found in Vat. Copt 59; see Toda, 283 and 285. Epiphanius,
Anacoratus 82, speaks of "certain ascetics of Egypt, of the Thebaid, and of other places,
who, following the Hieracites, deny the identity of the resurrected flesh with our own
flesh"; see K. Holl, Die grieschichen christlichen Shriftsteller, 25 (Leipzig, 1915),
102.30–103.4. Guillaumont, *Kephalaia Gnostica* 55, identifies these persons as Origenists, but this seems questionable. On Hieracas, see most recently James E.
Goehring, "Hieracas of Leontopolis: The Making of a Desert Ascetic," in his *Ascetics,
Society, and the Desert*, 110–33, esp. 125–30.

[68]A village in the Fayum. The Gk does not give the name of the village but situ-
ates Hieracas in the region of Arsinoë.

[69]*Oupna mputhos* = Gk *pneuma puthōna* (Acts 16:16).

[70]See *Life of Antony* 31–32.

[71]"Erroneous" and "led away" render forms of the same Coptic word, *sōrem*, "to
go astray, err."

which say that our[72] Lord Jesus Christ did not assume human flesh but
a heavenly flesh that he brought when he came to earth. They say that
there is no resurrection of the flesh for human beings.[73] They also say
that there are three principles, God, Matter, and Evil, and on account
of this they dare to say with certainty that the Logos of God did not
descend into humanity nor did he become completely human in everything human[74] except sin alone [Heb 4:15]. They say that [246] the
Logos of God was not the cause of creation [Jn 1:3]. They say that
through free will all human beings choose for themselves evil and thinking and acting like animals.

But in order not to proceed with a multitude of words about this
heresy, let me simply say that that man led a multitude of souls astray:
he led astray five hundred souls, both men and women. Indeed, he
rejected[75] marriage, saying that no man marrying a woman would
enter the kingdom of God; as a result, he caused a multitude of men
to leave their wives and a multitude of women to leave their hus-
bands.[76] Indeed, they believed in him because he said that the Spirit
had entrusted them to him, telling people[77] events that had not yet
taken place and they would take place. In a word, he controlled them
through these predictions. Indeed, if all the people's possessions were
lost, he would say to them, "Go to a certain place and you will find
them," and they would go[78] and find them. He would also tell them
when war was going to take place and how many people were going to
die and it happened just as he had said. Furthermore, he would cast out
other demons from people, and fulfilled in himself the words of the Lord
in the Gospel: "They will produce signs and wonders so they can lead

[72]b: our Lord; c: the Lord.

[73]b: *nte nirōmi*; c: *nnirōmi*. This teaching is corroborated by the *Life of Epiphanius* 27 (PG 41.57B-60A) and Epiphanius *Panarion* 67.1.5.

[74]b: *ni rōmi*; c: *ti metrōmi*.

[75]b: *nafhioui*; c: *afhioui*.

[76]See Athanasius' first *Letter to Virgins* (Brakke, 274–91, esp, 282–84), where he
attacks Hieracas' statement that "marriage is evil inasmuch as virginity is good."

[77]b: *nhanrōmi*; c: *nnirōmi*.

[78]b: *shauhōl*; c: *ouoh shauhōl*.

astray even my chosen ones" [Mt 24:24]. *Indeed, a demonic[79] spirit had possession of him; as a result, the demons obeyed him. Indeed, the demons agreed to work together in this[80] in order to induce vainglory and haughtiness on all sides so that a multitude of souls might perish with him.*

Therefore the bishop of Boushēm[81] came with his clergy to see Abba Macarius the man of God. They implored him,[82] "For God's sake help us. Please, take the trouble and bother; come where he lives so you can see what it is appropriate to do. If you do not purify our diocese[83] [247] *from this growing error,[84] all of Egypt will readily follow after it, for truly they are going astray when they see its signs and deeds."*

Abba Macarius said to the bishop, "I have decided to come with you. You know that I am an ignorant man and that I do not know what I will say to him. What, then, do you want me to say to him?"

The bishop fervently implored him, saying, "I believe that if you come with us, God will give peace to his Church. Indeed, often I have gotten ready to come to you concerning this matter but my clergy stopped me, saying, 'The world[85] will laugh at you.' Now, then, I have been unable to see[86] the destruction of the people and I fear danger encroaching against me[87] since God says, 'I will seek their blood from your hands' [Ezek 3:20]. *Therefore, I have come because God sent me to you."*

---

[79]Coptic/Gk: *archontikon*, which originally meant "ruling," then "angelic," but came to be used most often of evil angels (see *LH* 22:9–10); in Gnostic thought, the term designated the seven evil angels that ruled the world. This sentence might also be translated "a ruling spirit was in him."

[80]b: *naihōb*, these things; c: *paihōb*.

[81]b: *boushēm*; c: *oushēm*.

[82]b: *efof*; c: *erof*.

[83]Coptic *thosh* can mean "province, district, nome," or "diocese."

[84]*Taiplanē ekonkh.* BV translate as *"cette erreur de ton vivant."*

[85]Literally: "the world of men." BV suggest "the whole world." The Coptic follows the Gk in using *kosmikos* which can suggest "worldly, secular," so I have used "the world," which suggests both "everybody" and "the worldly."

[86]*Mpishnau.* Should this be "I do not wish to see"?

[87]b: *etkhajōri*; c: *et che khajōi.*

The old man got up right away and walked with them[88] and they stood outside the dwelling of that deceiver.[89] When the old man saw him at a distance, he said to the bishop, "A demonic spirit[90] is at work in this man.[91] You should know that this matter is outside my ken[92] for I have never done battle against great spirits like this. For our fathers told us that there are two orders of demons: one order[93] pours pleasure into people's bodies and the other order pours error into the soul. To be sure, this second [248] is difficult to defeat, while the first, the demons that attack the body, is very easy to humiliate. Satan has prepared these two orders. He has sent these two herds[94] and has commanded that whoever they lead astray becomes a heretic[95] and that they humiliate him by means of a delusion in order to destroy a multitude on account of him. These orders, therefore, are the friend of the leaders of heretical errors and magic-making sorcerers (especially wizards) and enchanters and diviners."

[96]*The bishop said, "What will we do, then, my father? We need great prayer from the depth of our hearts, for words will be ineffective." And he ordered them to call him outside.*

When he came out to them, the old man[97] strode confidently up to him with a mild look on his face; he greeted him and said to him, "Why

[88]b: *nsōou;* c: *nsōf.*

[89]b: *pikhello,* the old man; ac: *piplanos,* which looks like the *lectio facilior,* but *pikhello* could have been repeated from the first line of the par. or written in anticipation of the beginning of the next sentence. BV prefer "ce vieillard."

[90]*-pneuma narchontikon;* see n. 79 above.

[91]Ms. a differs considerably at the beginning of this paragraph: And the saint walked, rejoicing, and he arrived at that deceiver's dwelling and stood outside and had them call to him from outside so he could speak with him. When he came out, the Spirit-bearing old man saw him at a distance and knew everything about him and said to the bishop, "A demonic spirit is at work in this man."

[92]b: *phai;* c: *phōi.* Agreeing with BV, "*afin que tu saches que ce n'est pas mon affaire,*" rather than Chaîne, "*afin que tu ne connaisses pas la chose telle qu'elle est.*"

[93]b: *khen;* c: *nte.*

[94]Coptic *ageli* = Gk *agelē,* used of a herd of swine in Mt 8:31 and Lk 8:33. Cyril of Alexandria, *Fragmenta comentarii in Lucam* 4:22 (PG 72.544A) uses the word for a band of demons.

[95]b: *nteferheresis,* rather than "in his heresy," c: *khen tefheresis.*

[96]Evelyn White's first fragment (1.125) begins here.

[97]In Gk, the bishop acts and the first exchange takes place between the bishop and the heretic.

haven't I seen you until today, and why haven't you paid us a visit?"

He said to the old man, *"I haven't paid you a visit because your faith is not firm."*

The man of God said to him, *"What about your faith? Are you orthodox?"*

He said to him, *"Quite orthodox."*

The man of God said to him, *"What is wrong or irregular about our faith?"*

He said to him, *"Your faith is not orthodox because you say that this flesh and this bone will rise. Not only that, but you also say that the Son of God took on*[98] *flesh and bone."*

The holy old man responded to him with dignity, saying, *"If we say these things by ourselves or if we have discovered them by means of our own intelligence, then you are right to find fault with us, but if Holy Scripture has given them to us, then what we do is right. If, therefore, the righteousness of God wishes it to be this way, why do you oppose God's ordinance? In order not to get off track with a lot of words, we will inform you about our faith.*[99] *If you agree with us, good; but if you do not agree with us, then your judgment is in God's hands and you are overthrowing* [249] *his ordinances in opposing him."*

He said to him,[100] *"I will explain my faith first."*

The old man said to him, *"We will not allow a wicked faith to be explained. No, we will explain our orthodox faith, the faith of the Catholic Church."*

And[101] the old man ordered the bishop to speak, and[102] while all the people stood,[103] the bishop spoke and first began to explain the

---

[98]b: *pshēri či*; a: *apshēri či*.

[99]Evelyn White's first fragment (1.125) ends here.

[100]b: *nak*; a: *naf*; -c.

[101]b: *auoh*; ac: *ouoh*.

[102]c+ *ouoh*.

[103]One notes that all the people stand and it is the bishop who recites the creed. The scene has a liturgical "feel" to it, one that resembles the *traditio symboli*, the "handing over of the creed" which was a rite during Lent for those preparing for baptism (at least in Jerusalem, Milan, Rome, and North Africa). See J. N. D. Kelly, *Early Christian Creeds* (London: Longmans, 1950).

orthodox faith, saying, "We believe in one God, God the Father
Almighty, creator of what is visible and invisible. We believe in his only-
begotten Son, the Logos of God, consubstantial with the Father, who
created everything through him [Jn 1:3]; who, at the end of time,
wanted to destroy sin and became human, complete in everything
according to our image except sin alone [Heb 4:15], having entered the
womb of the Virgin Mary; who was crucified and died in the flesh; who
rose on the third day. He ascended to the heights in heaven and sat at
the right side of his Father. He will come to judge the living and the
dead. We believe in the Holy Spirit, who is consubstantial with the
Father and the Son.[104] We also believe there is a resurrection of the soul
and of the body,[105] according to the word of the apostle: 'It is sown a
physical body; it will be raised a spiritual body' [1 Cor 15:44], and 'It is
necessary that this death put on deathlessness and that this corrupt-
ibility put on incorruptibility' [1 Cor 15:53]. You see, therefore, how he
speaks about this corruption."[106]

That heretic[107] and deceiver said, "I am not seeking a merely[108]
verbal faith, but if your faith is orthodox, [250] let it be shown through
works and mighty deeds. Let us go to the tombs, therefore, and there
raise for me someone from the dead and if you raise someone from the

---

[104]It is unusual that the term *homoousios* ("consubstantial") is applied here to the
Holy Spirit; the term is not used for the Spirit in either the Nicene or Constantinop-
olitan creeds. Interestingly, Athanasius did apply the key Nicene term to the Spirit, in
Letter to Serapion 1.25: "Because he [the Spirit] is one, and still more, because he is
proper to the Word who is one, he is proper to God who is one, and one in essence
[*homoousios*] with him." See also *Letter to Serapion* 2.6. Athanasius, however (like Basil
of Caesarea), did not call the Spirit "God." See Hanson, *Search for the Christian Doctrine of God*, 748–53.

[105]Or: with (*nem*) the body.

[106]a: You see how he is saying that this corruption is that which will return incor-
ruptible in the resurrection, with glory, if the person is righteous [see 1 Cor 15:52–54].
BV, 113 n. 49, correct Chaîne's citation from "I (*ti*) see" to "you (*ch*) see." On the general issue of the resurrection of the body in the theology of the early Church, see Brian
E. Daley, *The Hope of the Early Church: A Handbook of Patristic Eschatology* (Cambridge: Cambridge University Press, 1991).

[107]Coptic/Gk: *asebēs*.

[108]c+ *mmauatf*.

dead, then we will know that your faith is orthodox.[109] *If not, I will pro-duce for you a soul without a body."*

Saint Abba Macarius looked at the bishop and said,[110] *"It is a great evil to tempt God on account of a single misled person in order to bring about this great sign."*

The bishop said to him, "It is not on account of a single person but rather a whole diocese with its city and villages."

They went to the tombs and Hieracas[111] *began to call out to*[112] *a demon, for in truth it is not possible to bring forth a soul that is naked, one without its body; rather, the demon assumed the shape of the soul in front of Hieracas until he deceived him. Although he called to the demon a long time, he was able to do nothing and stopped, for the Holy Spirit who indwelt Abba Macarius the Great prevented him from doing anything. When the heretic was put to shame, he said to them, "It is because of your lack of faith that I am not able to produce a soul."*

And Saint Abba Macarius stood firm in the Holy Spirit and his spirit burned. He single-mindedly threw himself to his knees and spent an hour submerged in prayer with the bishop and the whole crowd that had accompanied them.[113] *He got up from the ground with the power of the Holy Spirit bestowed on him by our Lord Jesus Christ, the Son of the living God, and knocked on the tomb with the staff made of palm branches that he carried in his hand*[114] *(the staffs of the monks are made from date-palm trees),*[115] *and while he struck the door of the tomb, he said,*[116] *"By the holy power of our Lord Jesus Christ, the Son of the living God, who came in human flesh and died in it and rose in it, he will also do this mighty deed!" And immediately the door of the*

---

[109]In *Life of Antony* 80.3 Antony makes a similar demand of the philosophers with whom he is debating.

[110]c+ *naf*.

[111]The follower of Hieracas is now mistakenly called "Hieracas" here and below.

[112]b: *ethbe*; ac: *oube*.

[113]b: *ethnemōu*; c: *ethnemaf*, him.

[114]b: *nefjij*; c: *tefjij*.

[115]See Evagrius *Praktikos* Prologue 7; Cassian *Institutes* 1.7–8; Cassian *Conferences* 11.3 (BV).

[116]These words, and the details that follow, are missing in Gk (BV).

tomb opened[117] [251] *and everyone saw the dead person bound forward until he reached the entrance. The saint ordered them to undo the bandages that bound him* [Jn 11:44]. *The dead man who had been raised stood up and spoke with them, saying,*[118]

[And he gave a knock on the tomb with the staff that he held in his hand and said, "In the name of the power of our Lord Jesus Christ, the Son of the Living God, who assumed human flesh from the holy Virgin Mary; he suffered among us for our salvation and died in the flesh and rose from the dead as God. It is you, my Lord Jesus Christ,[119] *who will do this mighty deed."*[120]

And suddenly the door of the tomb opened and they saw the dead man come forward until he reached the entrance of the tomb, and immediately Saint Abba Macarius ordered them to loosen the wrappings with which he was bound [Jn 11:44]. *And moreover that day was the 22nd of Pharmouthi* [March 19] *in the 82nd year of Diocletian* [A.D. 366] *and it took place in the 362nd year since the economy of Christ, as the zealous servants of God who were with him that day told us.*

What a great miracle this was! Or, rather, it was the power of God with which God had graced this holy man on account of his good works,[121] *for who would be able to say that this miracle was different from those that the apostles did or was inferior to them? Indeed, this great saint Abba Macarius was himself an apostle in the way he emulated them through the evangelical works that he established which were like those of the apostles. But let us proceed to the conclusion of this miracle that took place through the great God-bearing and blessed saint Abba Macarius. The one who had been raised from the dead stood and said to them,]*

---

[117]**b**: *ouōnh*; **ac**: *ouōn*.

[118]and knocked . . . saying: **a** (124v–125r; Chaîne, 251) differs considerably, so I have placed it in brackets.

[119]Chaîne prints *pačsīhšpjš*, which must be a mistake for *pačsīhšpčhš*. BV translate "*mon Seigneur.*"

[120]"Mighty deed" and "power" both translate *jom*.

[121]See the *Life of Macarius of Scetis* 29 for a similar statement and emphasis on the power of God.

"Blessed be God who has brought my soul [252] *above from Hades below* [Ps 86:13] *so I can see this light again!*"

They said to him, "What generation are you? Did you know Christ, or not?"

The dead man said, "I belong to an ancient generation from the time of the kings of Antioch; I am a pagan who does not know God [1 Th 4:5, Gal 4:8]. But while I was in punishment, suddenly a royal personage came down where I was; there was a golden crown on his head and going before him was a cross of gold. That king whom I saw I recognize today, standing and commanding his friend and saying, 'Lazarus, come, bring this soul and place it in its former body and give it to Macarius the righteous because he is standing there today before my judgment seat'" [Rom 14:10, 2 Cor 5:10. On Lazarus, see Jn 11:1–44].

When the man who had been raised had spoken, Abba Macarius spoke to Hieracas, "Ask this man who has been raised whether or not those who have died and who will rise again have flesh." And when the heretic stood refuted, his demon fled and left him, filled with shame, for he saw the great sign. He threw himself to the ground, therefore, and worshipped God, kissing the feet of the holy man Abba Macarius with the whole crowd in prayer.

The crowd was trying to get their hands on him in order to kill him but the old man would not allow them to do it but instead took him with him into his cell in the interior desert. Hieracas practiced asceticism with Abba Macarius with great repentance and with abundant tears and when he had spent three years doing acts of penance for God, God put his body at ease[122] while he diligently practiced asceticism with the aid of the holy prayers of Abba Macarius the Great.[123]

As for the man who had been raised from the dead, Abba Macarius took him to the cell where his disciples lived[124] and he baptized him in his church because he had said "I am a pagan who does not know Christ." And he entrusted him to his disciples until the repentance of

---

[122]*Chaf ebol* can also mean "forgive."
[123]b: *nieuchē ethouab nte*; a: *nieuchē nte ethouab*.
[124]b:*hemsi*; c lacks.

Hieracas was completed. When he died [253] and was buried, the old man transferred his remains to his church.[125] *He took the man who had been raised under his direction for three years and instructed him with determination*[126] *until he successfully completed his life and died. He lived six years, having gone to his rest in good repose*[127] *so that the word of Christ was fulfilled*[128] *concerning him: "Neither this man nor his parents*[129] *sinned but . . . in order that the glory of God might be revealed in him"* [Jn 9:3].[130]

[And yet another thing happened in the tomb: the stone that was placed at the entrance of the tomb that Saint Abba Macarius had knocked on with the palm-tree staff in his hand rolled away by itself from the entrance of the tomb where he had approached and stood, and no one has been able to move it inside from there since the day that God placed it with another tomb as a sign for everyone who wanted to see it.][131]

A little later the bishop asked the old man Abba Macarius, saying, "My father, do not conceal your thoughts from me. Did human glory enter your heart when all these people worshipped you on account of the great sign that took place through you?"

Abba Macarius said to him, "For the person whose heart[132] *rests in God, united with him at all times, it is not possible for human glory to bind itself to him nor enter his heart. As for the person into whose heart human glory ascends, that person has not known God. What he does is human.*[133] *The person who seeks to please people ceases to please God*

---

[125]b: *etekklēsia*; ac: *etefekklēsia*. See the prior sentence. See n. 59 above.

[126]b: *oumetjarhēt*; c: *oumetjafhēt*.

[127]See 1 Tim 1:18, 1 Tim 6:12, 2 Tim 4:7 for this construction (BV).

[128]"Fulfilled" and "completed" both translate *jōk*.

[129]b: *nefioti*; c: *nefkeioti*.

[130]The editor has omitted "he was born blind" from Jn 9:3 (indicated by the ellipses), the omission of which fits his purpose but jars the syntax.

[131]a (127r-127v) adds.

[132]b: *pefhēt*; c: *pefmeui*, his thought.

[133]a (128r) has a much shorter version of Macarius' speech from this point to the end: "The person who acts on account of human glory, seeking to please people, in behaving this way ceases from pleasing the Lord and is mocked in battle and falls from virtue and loses what he has gained through hard work because he has acted according to human values."

and has been mocked in battle and has fallen from virtue. But[134] *the person who has been worthy to receive right knowledge of God while locked in a great struggle, fearful of losing the fervor that unites him with God, is like someone standing on* [254] *a dancer's mast:*[135] *if he turns the slightest bit he will fight and fall. He never even has any concern of leaving his body because his desire is to leave his body and be with Christ* [Phil 1:23]. *As for human glory, it never enters his heart; or rather, he shuns it as an antelope would. Indeed, it seems to us that this human glory is vain and transitory.*

"I will give you an analogy that will explain this matter to you:[136] *It is like a person who stands on the waters of the sea looking at the sun in the sky above, held aloft by means of its rays. If he removes his gaze from the sun, which is holding him aloft by means of its rays, and looks at the waters that he treads upon, will he not sink because he has turned his gaze from the heights of the sun that holds him aloft by means of its rays? What will happen to him because he has disobeyed the sun who says to him, 'Do not look at the waters nor cease gazing at me; it is not you holding yourself aloft but my rays'? So too is it with the person whose view is united with God, who seeks always the glory of God: he tramples underfoot all human glory. But if he turns toward human glory, he falls from the glory of God and his sight. He defiles himself by means of a multitude of different passions so that in the end he sinks with all his cargo."*

The bishop was amazed and marveled at his speech and his subtle understanding. [255] *He returned to his village in peace, having profited, glorifying God.*[137]

---

[134]c+ *de*.

[135]*Outhok nkoreus.* Gk has "razor," but *thok* also means "razor" (Crum 403a). See Cassian *Conferences* 23.9.1: "Rightly then would I say that holy persons, who keep firm hold of the recollection of God and are as it were carried along on their lofty way by lines stretched out on high, should be compared to funambulists, popularly called tightrope walkers" (Ramsey, 799–800).

[136]b: *mmok*; c: *mmoi*. Evelyn White's second fragment (1.126) begins with the next sentence.

[137]a (128r) adds: "There were in addition many other wonders even greater than these and numerous healings that he accomplished through God's grace that we have

Abba Macarius Heals a Young Man Possessed by a Demon (LH *17.11*)

7   An old woman came to him one time bringing him her son *bound in iron fetters*, detained by two men, *for this young man was possessed by a madly raging demon.*[138] His mother *was walking behind him*, weeping. This was what that demon was doing: after eating three measures[139] of bread and drinking a jug of water[140] *each day*, he would vomit and all the food would disintegrate *like smoke* and the food would be consumed like a fire[141] *devouring stubble.*[142] And the food that he ate each day was not enough for him[143] but he would turn even to his excrement: he would eat[144] it and also drink his urine.[145] *For this reason the two men had bound him in order to stop him from eating even his excrement, and he would try to escape from them so he could tear up his clothes and eat*[146] *them* [Lk 8:29]. *If they allowed him firewood or some other combustible or if he found them on the ground, he felt great shame [sic].*[147]

---

not ‹written› [emending *nnensshe* to *nnenskhai*] at greater length in this book because they are written in the book of his way of life which the man of God Saint Jerome has made known." Evelyn White's second fragment (1.126) lacks this addition. One ms., LIX, of the *Life of Macarius of Scetis* 32 contains this statement.

[138]See Jerome *Life of Hilarion* 10.1–2, 5–6 (BV).

[139]Coptic *ment*, less than an *ertob*; Chaîne suggests that it equals Gk *modios* (Mt 5:5, Mk 4:21, Lk 11:33), about eight quarts.

[140]Evelyn White's second fragment (1.126), which has included all the Coptic additions in 7 (in italics in the text above), breaks off here.

[141]There may be a play on sound here: "fire" renders *chrōm* while "smoke" translates *chremte*.

[142]Gk +: "For there is a class of demons called fiery, since demons have differences just as men do, not of essence but of knowledge" (Meyer, 57).

[143]Gk +: "from his own mother."

[144]b: *shafouomou*; c: *ntefouomou*.

[145]For examples of similar behavior, see *Life of Antony* 64.1 (Evagrius' Latin version) and Cassian *Conferences* 7.27 (BV).

[146]b: *ntefouōm*; c: *efouōm*.

[147]This seems to be a confused repetition of the earlier "after eating three measures of bread and drinking a jug of water *each day*, he would vomit and all the food would disintegrate *like smoke* and the food would be consumed like a fire *devouring stubble.*"

His mother threw herself at the feet of Saint Abba Macarius,[148] weeping and pleading with him, *saying, "Help me in my widowhood and my feebleness! This is my only child and this evil demon has taken control of him."*[149]

He said to her, "Be patient, old woman. I believe that God will take [256] *pity on you and your little one. Therefore be patient a few days."*

The saint ordered them to lay him in a cell inside the hospital and there cover his mouth so he could not eat and[150] drink. The saint used to heal a multitude of people at all times; five or six recovered their health every day on account of his prayers. As a result, there was not enough water in the cistern for the crowds that came to him each day.

I myself saw the place where the sick lay;[151] the place lay at a distance of a third of a stadion from the church.[152]

Macarius' Secret Tunnel (LH 17.10)

8   *Since it was necessary*[153] *for him to take the road to see those who were*[154] *sick in order to pray for them,*[155] *and* since the crowds bothered him, he dug in the earth below the church[156] and made a tunnel that he took to the hospice for the sick.[157] He would travel it beneath the earth twice a day to see them[158] by means of the hidden passage (no one knew about it), saying twenty-four prayers while walking to see them under the earth and twenty-four prayers *with*

[148]b: *nabba makarios piagios*; c: *piagios abba makarios*. Gk: the saint.

[149]The Gk from here to the end differs completely (see *LH* 17.12–13; Meyer, 57–58); see par. 9 below for the conclusion of the story.

[150]ac+ ouoh.

[151]c+ nkot.

[152]About 70 yards.

[153]b: *nakagkē*; ac: *nanagkē*.

[154]b: *phmōit nnē*; c: *phmōit nte nē*.

[155]b: *ejōou*; c: *ehrēi ejōou*.

[156]Gk omits the part about the church and says that the tunnel ran from his cell for about half a mile and that he dug it "over a long period of time."

[157]Instead of a hospice, Gk says that the tunnel ended in a cave.

[158]that . . . them: a lacks.

metanoia[159] while returning *from them under the earth until he came to his church.*[160] *And in this way he would visit them twice a day, praying with them and petitioning God to heal them.*

Macarius Rebukes the Widow for her Lack of Charity
(LH 17.12–13)[161]

9   After twenty days he opened the door of the young man's cell, brought him out, and undid his fetters because in truth the demon had left him, and the man of God spoke to the young man's mother,[162] "How many loaves of bread would you have your son eat *each day?*"

She said to him,[163] "I would have him eat ten pounds[164] of bread a day."

The old man *grew angry and* rebuked her, saying, "The amount you're saying is too much, *but if you have more than you need, give seven pounds each day to the helpless widows and give the other three pounds to your son* [257] *every day.*[165] See here! By the grace of God, from now on your son will eat only three pounds of bread each day so he can do a little manual labor.[166] *But listen, and I will also tell you how this demon got power over your son.*[167] *His father died and left you a few necessities, more than you needed to live, and there were old*

---

[159]A *metanoia* at this period was probably an act of prostration.

[160]Gk says that one of Macarius' "earnest disciples" told the author about the prayers.

[161]See par. 7 above for the first part of this story.

[162]After . . . mother: Gk, "And after one or two days, when the fever had abated, blessed Macarius asked her."

[163]c lacks *naf.*

[164]Coptic *lutra* = Gk, *litra*, 12 ounces, therefore seven and a half of our pounds.

[165]Five and a quarter and two and a quarter pounds, respectively.

[166]See here . . . labor: Gk, "He prayed over the young man and fasted for the space of seven days; then he put the young man on a diet of three pounds and obliged him to do some work." Three pounds = two and a quarter pounds.

[167]See HM 30.2.1–3 (= Gk 22.3–4) (BV).

women, widows—*poor, powerless, and infirm—who were your neigh-*
bors and were in need of alms and you gave them nothing. Because of
this, God allowed this demon to enter your son so he would eat your
goods and dissipate them through his insatiable appetite so you your-
selves would become poor[168] *because you would not give alms to the*
infirm."

And in this way he taught them to give alms, having given the
young man back to his mother, *healed, praying to God and giving*
thanks to Christ while his thoughts were firmly fixed on the Lord. And
everyone who heard gave glory to God who glorifies and exalts his saints
who love him with all their hearts.

God did this other miracle through Abba Macarius. I did not see
it with my own eyes[169] because in truth he went to his rest before[170]
I entered the monastic settlement,[171] *but his disciples told me about*
the mighty deeds that God did through him.

Abba Macarius and Abba Amoun[172]

10 *They also told me this story: Abba Macarius told us that there was*
an old man named Abba Amoun who was a neighbor of Abba Antony
in the interior desert.[173] *The old man paid a visit to Abba Antony one*
time. When he entered the cell, they prayed, sat down, and discussed a
question.[174] *The old man*[175] *said to Abba Antony, "Why is my labor*
greater than yours but your name is so great among the people? No one
knows that I'm alive."

[168]A wry etymology occurs here: "poor," *hēki*, comes from the root word *hko*, "hungry," so the young man was quite literally eating them into hungry poverty.

[169]I . . . eyes: Gk, "I did not meet him."

[170]Gk: "a year before."

[171]*LH* 17 ends here.

[172]Although absent from the *LH*, this story may be found, in a shorter version, in *AP* Amoun 1.

[173]See *Life of Antony* 60. On Amoun, see Evelyn White 2.45–50.

[174]Literally "struck or cast a thought," *auhioui noumeui. Hioui* seems unusual here; BV translate "*étudièrent une question.*"

[175]**b**: *pičello*; **ac**: *pikhello*.

Abba Antony said to him, "But I love [258] God more than you."[176]

The old man said to him, "How do you love God more than I? I have left everything behind and I've taken on greater labors than you."

Abba Antony said to him, "Believe me. So great is the love in my heart for God that if my thoughts turn away from him for even a little, I weep like little children when their mother lays them down and hides herself a little while until she sees her children's love for her."

The old man replied and said,[177] *"Woe is me! I do not know that a single tear has ever fallen from my eyes, from the day I became a monk up to today. Pray for me; perhaps the Lord will have mercy on me."*

The Mighty Deeds and Virtues of Abba Macarius

11   *With regard to the rest of the mighty deeds and virtues of Saint Abba Macarius the Egyptian, what sort they were, how he was so compassionate, and how he kept such close watch over himself, if I*[178] *were to recount all of them, I would unduly lengthen this account. But I will cease narrating here the lofty works of Abba Macarius, who was so perfect in righteousness that it is impossible to gather together all the healings that the Lord worked through him and his numerous ascetic practices, especially since other works of his are written in other books.*

The Death of Abba Macarius[179]

12   *Abba Paphnutius, the disciple of Abba Macarius, said that when Christ the King came to visit Abba Macarius and take*[180] *his body from*

---

[176]*AP* Amoun 1 ends here.

[177]c lacks *pejaf.*

[178]b: *aishanphiri;* c: *anshanphiri.*

[179]BV 121 (see n. 80) switch to Amélineau's text here (104–11), but I will continue with Chaîne's text, with Vogüé's notes. BV give a French translation of this paragraph on 126 (D). See *Life of Macarius of Scetis* 35.

[180]b: *etafenf;* c: *afenf.*

this world in order to give him rest from the sweat and labors he had accepted for the sake of immortality in[181] *life eternal, while some of the saints who had come to see him were standing* [259] *over his precious*[182] *remains, at that time he glowed with fire and they saw his blessed soul seized and taken through the gateway of life. They saw those in the air gathered together in great commotion, and suddenly they cried out before him with loud voices, "You have come, Macarius!"*

He replied to them, "I am not yet able[183] *to trust*[184] *or believe what you are saying."*[185] *In saying these things, he stepped through the gate.*

Once again they cried out, "You have come, Macarius!"

And Abba Macarius lifted his voice on high with a loud voice of angelic rejoicing and celebration so that the earth resounded with the sound,[186] *"Blessed be the Eternal One, whose mercy is great, whom my soul has loved, for I sought and I have found, I knocked and the King of Glory,*[187] *the true God, Christ,*[188] *has opened for me the way to eternal life;*[189] *he has deemed me worthy of heavenly freedom from the snares you [(pl.) sic] have dug for humanity."*

When he had said these things, the just judge [2 Tim 4:8], *who rewards those who stand in fear before him and who love his gospel well, hid him from them.*

Glory to the Father and to the Son and to the Holy Spirit.[190]

---

[181]b: *etkhen*; c: *nte.*
[182]b: *etaiēout*; c: *ethouab.*
[183]b: *mpatishcha*; c: *mpaticha.*
[184]b: *pahēt*; c: *pihēt.*
[185]Text: *naisali*, which must be a misprint for *naisaji.*
[186]b: *tismē*; c: *tefsmē.*
[187]c adds p̄c̄h̄s̄.
[188]c lacks p̄c̄h̄s.
[189]See Mt 7:7 and Ps 24:8.
[190]a lacks this doxology.

[THE SHORT RECENSION][191]

Abba Macarius Saves a Woman Changed into a Mare (LH 17.6–9)[192]

1 (5) [271] An Egyptian fell in love with a free woman[193] who had a husband. He was unable[194] to sport with her and went to a sorcerer's shop and entreated him, "Either get her to love me or let *there be enmity between her and* her husband *so that he* repudiates her." So the sorcerer received a large amount of money from him and worked his evil craft and caused the woman to have the appearance of a mare. When her husband saw her, he was astonished and said, "How has this mare climbed into my bed? *What is going on here?*" The man spoke with the mare, weeping *with great suffering,* but she did not answer him. The man got up and went to find the priests of the village and brought them inside his home. They saw her and did not know what was the matter. Three days passed without her eating anything: she neither ate fodder like a mare nor did she eat bread like a woman but was deprived of food.

In the end, however, this took place so God might be glorified and so the virtue of *Abba* Macarius the Great[195] might be revealed. This thought occurred to her husband: "Go to the desert where the man of God lives," and [272] her husband rose and bridled her like a ‹horse›[196] and led her to the desert. When he drew near where the

---

[191]Translated from M. Chaîne, "La double recension," 271–73, with additional textual material supplied by Adalbert de Vogüé, "La version copte." Abbreviations: **a** = Vat. Copt 59, **b** = Vat. Copt 62, **c** = Vat. Copt 64.

[192]Section titles are my own. Portions in italics are lacking in Gk. Paragraphs without "*LH*" in parentheses lack parallels with the *Lausiac History*. Paragraph numbers do not correspond to *LH* but are given for ease of reference. Numbers in parentheses indicate paragraph numbers of the long recension above and numbers in brackets give the pagination of Chaîne's text.

[193]Coptic lacks "of good position." See n. 51 above.

[194]Reading with Vogüé *mpefjemjom* instead of *ete mptērf jemjom.*

[195]Gk: the holy Macarius.

[196]Text: dog. Chaîne points out that the scribe mistakenly wrote *ouhor* (dog) instead of *hthōr* (horse).

brothers were standing beside the church[197] of Abba Macarius, they quarreled with the man, "You there, why have you brought this mare here?"

The man answered, "In order that pity might be taken on her."

The brothers said, "Why?"

He said to them, "She's my wife. I don't know what's happened to her. She's turned into a mare and has tasted nothing for three days."

They left and told the old man. They found him praying,[198] making intercession on her behalf. Abba Macarius[199] replied to them and said, "It's you, rather, who are horses, who have the eyes of horses. She could not have been changed into a mare unless tricks were being played on people's eyes."

He blessed some water and poured it over her from her head down and prayed over her and immediately he caused her to look like a woman *in front of all of them.* And he brought her some bread, which she ate, and he dismissed her with her husband. She gave thanks to God and he gave her this command: "Do not ever stay away from church[200] and not receive the mysteries; *do not ever stop attending the synaxis where one drinks the cup.* All these things happened to you because you stopped receiving the holy mysteries for five weeks."

And so they went home, glorifying God.

Abba Macarius Heals a Young Man Possessed by a Demon (LH 17.11)

2 (7) One time he was brought a young man possessed by a demon; his mother was *walking behind him,* weeping, and two *other young* men had hold of him *so he could not escape.* And this [273] was how

[197]Gk: "cell."
[198]Coptic lacks: "for God had revealed this to him."
[199]Gk: "the holy Macarius."
[200]Literally: "remain outside."

that demon acted: after the young man ate three measures[201] of bread and drank a *kilikision*[202] of water from a pot,[203] he would vomit. The food[204] would dissipate *like smoke*; in this way he made like fire all the food and water that he vomited. There is also an order of fiery demons [since demons have differences] just as human beings do, [not of essence but] of knowledge.[205]

The young man, therefore, was never satisfied with everything he ate, but would turn and eat his excrement and drink his urine. His mother wept *in great sadness* and beseeched the *holy* saint *of God, Abba* Macarius. And the blessed[206] old man *rose and* prayed and[207] beseeched God on her behalf[208] and after a day or two the young man was released from the demon through the prayers of the old man.[209] And *the man of God*, Saint Abba Macarius,[210] addressed the young man's mother, "How much bread would you have your son eat *a day?*"

She said, "I would have him eat ten pounds[211] *of bread a day*."

The old man rebuked her and the old man said to her, "The amount you've said is too much," and he prayed for him while fasting.[212] He apportioned three pounds[213] *of bread a day* for him so he could work and thus he returned him safe and sound[214] to his mother.

---

[201]Coptic *ment*, less than an *ertob*; Chaîne suggests that it equals Gk *modios* (Mt 5:5, Mk 4:21, Lk 11:33), about eight quarts.

[202]The same term is used in *LH* 17.11; see Lampe 753B and G. J. M. Bartelink, ed., *Palladio: La Storia Lausiaca* (Milan: Fondazione Lorenzo Valla, 1974), 334.

[203]Coptic -*lakon*. BV suggest that *lakon* = Gk *lekanē* (= *lekos*), "dish, pot, pan" (LSJ 1037AB). The word recurs in the *Life of Macarius of Alexandria*.

[204]*Nikhrēibi* = *nikhroui*, as Chaîne suggests.

[205]The Coptic omits a number of words, supplied from the Gk.

[206]b: *efsmarōout*; a: *etsmarōut*.

[207]b: *suoh*; a: *ouoh*.

[208]Gk: "for him."

[209]The young man . . . the old man: Gk, "when the fever had abated."

[210]Gk: "blessed Macarius."

[211]*Litra*, twelve ounces; so seven and a half of our pounds.

[212]Coptic lacks "for seven days."

[213]That is, two and a quarter pounds.

[214]Coptic *ouoj* also suggests "saved."

They went home with great joy, glorifying God, marvelling at the acts of grace that God did through the blessed old man and the numerous healings that took place through him. We will now cease . . . .[215]

---

[215]The text breaks off here.

CHAPTER FOUR

The Life of Macarius of Alexandria (*Lausiac History* 18)

INTRODUCTION

Saint Macarius of Alexandria

Macarius of Alexandria is a much less prominent figure than Macarius of Egypt (the Great). The alphabetical collection of the *Apophthegmata* attributes only three sayings to the former while giving forty-one apophthegms to the latter, more than anyone else except Poemen;[1] the *Historia Monachorum* devotes about five times as much space to the Egyptian as to the Alexandrian.[2] The *Lausiac History*, however, gives Macarius of Alexandria more than double the space of Macarius the Great; the chapter devoted to the former is the book's longest. The Coptic text, though truncated at the beginning, expands the chapter even more.

One does not have to search far for the reason. In the opening of chapter 18 of the *Lausiac History* (missing unfortunately from the Coptic manuscript), Palladius declares:

I met the other Macarius, however [Macarius the Great had died the year before Palladius came to the desert], the one

---

[1]But see A. Guillaumont, "Le problème," on the confusion of the two Macarii in the *Apophthegmata*.
[2]Chapters 21 and 23 respectively.

from Alexandria, a priest of so-called Cellia, where I stayed
for nine years, and he was actually alive during three of those
years. Some of the things I saw, others I heard about, and
some I learned about from others.[3]

The Coptic version of the *Life* continues this eyewitness reportage,
and even expands on it (see below). From this account, two domi-
nant themes emerge: Macarius the Ascetic and Macarius the Mira-
cleworker.[4]

Macarius' asceticism can be summarized perhaps by two sayings
unique to the Coptic text (pars. 12 and 13; par. 12 is corroborated by
Evagrius Ponticus) and one saying shared by both Coptic and Greek
texts (par. 4 = *LH* 18.10): he told the following "in the presence of the
young brothers in order to prompt their emulation: 'From the day
that I became a monk I have not eaten my fill of bread and I have not
slept as much as I could.'"[5] "He told us this other saying concerning
himself: When he was young, he spent an entire year without putting
on any clothing except for an old rag wrapped around his loins and
his members." Macarius' dwelling places could be as severe as his
clothing and eating habits. Although the Coptic and Greek versions
vary on the locales of Macarius' cells, they agree that "some of them
were without doors, for in truth they were located in the interior
desert where he did not encounter anyone: these were where he lived
during the season of Lent, *dark caves lying beneath the earth, similar
to hyenas' dens*; indeed, they were so narrow that he was not able to
straighten out his limbs at all" (italicized words are lacking in Greek).

Not surprisingly, Macarius desired to be perfect (a common
theme in early monastic literature): "Every ascetic practice that I had
undertaken I had successfully completed, but the desire also entered

---

[3]*LH* 18.1 (Meyer, 58, altered). For *par' heterōn mamathēka* ("I learned about from
others") Meyer translates "had by hearsay."

[4]Antoine Guillaumont has noted, "Le problème," 54, that "Macarius is a virtuoso
of asceticism, but even in his asceticism there is a sense of humor."

[5]See *Praktikos* 94 (Bamberger, trans., 40). Gabriel Bunge, "Évagre le Pontique et
les deux Macaires," regards this Macarius as Macarius of Alexandria (see 221–22, 223).

my heart to do this: I wanted to spend five days with my heart focused on God at all times without paying any attention at all to the ways of this age." He retreated to his cell "in the interior desert, the one without door or window or any light, so no one could find" him and fought with demons for five days. At the end of that time, he learned a valuable lesson: "I was unable to master my thought without distraction but I returned to worldly worries and human ways of seeing. I understood that if I was going to succeed in completing [my desire for perfection], I would destroy my understanding and become insanely arrogant. For this reason I was at peace allowing the cares of this world into my heart so I would not fall into arrogance" (par. 8; *LH* 18.17–18).

Macarius' deep asceticism is tempered by and inseparable from awe and compassion. The "mysteries," sacraments, are exactly that, a mystery. Macarius tells his disciple that "at the time of the mysteries . . . I did not give the sacrament to Mark the Ascetic a single time but when he came to receive communion I would see an angel placing the sacrament in his hands" (par. 16; *LH* 18.25). His sense of wonder extended to his own priestly duties at the altar; again he tells his disciple, "Not a Saturday or a Sunday passed that I did not see the angel of the altar standing in front of me as I celebrated the Holy Communion of God." Macarius' sense of awe undoubtedly combined with an appreciation of God's awesome power; there is no cheap grace with Macarius. When Palladius and Albinus, tender-hearted at the sight of a priest whose scalp is eaten away by cancer, beg Abba Macarius to help the cleric, Macarius harshly responds, "Let him be; he doesn't deserve to be healed, for in truth although he stopped fornicating he still went up to the altar" (par. 9; *LH* 18.19–21). The priest spent three days imploring Macarius; "finally, he took pity on his tears and his supplication" and healed him—but only after he got the priest to promise to give up his presbyteral office.

For Macarius, sternness and compassion bring together mercy *and* justice; both are necessary. The delightful story of the hyena pup illustrates this well (par. 2; *LH* 18.27–28). A hyena brings her cub to

Macarius to heal. After he does so, she rewards him with a sheepskin "very plush and soft."[6] Macarius is not pleased, though: "Where did you get this unless you ate a sheep?" he demands. "What you have brought me has come from violence. I will not accept it from you." The hyena hits her head on the ground and bends her paws, "imploring him like a person" to take the sheepskin from her. But Macarius reiterates that he will "not accept the sheepskin unless you promise me not to hurt the poor by eating their sheep." Macarius gets her promise and tells her she may eat only carrion; if she can not find food, she must come to him and he will feed her bread. The hyena returns to her lair and comes to visit Abba Macarius, and Macarius gives thanks to God. "The old man," Palladius concludes, "slept on the sheepskin until his death. I saw it with my own eyes." In an ending reminiscent of the *Life of Antony*, when Macarius "was about to die, Melania . . . happened to pay him a visit. He gave that sheepskin to her as an inheritance. It remained in her possession until her death; she faithfully kept it as a remembrance."[7]

It is all too easy to dismiss such a story, with its anthropomorphisms and folk simplicity, as naive, but Macarius understands the story's import, and he gives thanks to God for it. "And the old man understood that it was the economy of God that gives intelligence even to wild beasts in order to teach us a lesson." Macarius understands that everything is part of God's economy, God's plan, and his actions indicate that he embodies both mercy and justice. At receiving the gift of the sheepskin from the hyena, Macarius' first thought is for the poor. Later in the *Life* (par. 11), he not only allows (foreign) robbers to steal all his possessions during a famine, he helps them and sees them on their way.[8] When some monks come to see him, he asks them to use their bread; he has none because, he says, "God

---

[6] Healings of animals are a common occurrence in the *Virtues of Saint Macarius*, which are about Macarius of Egypt.

[7] *Life of Antony* 92.

[8] Similar stories are told about Macarius of Egypt; see *AP* Macarius the Great 40 and 18.

has given the bodily necessities that were here in my dwelling to some men of the world who have wives because some poor folk needed them due to the severity of the famine." Asceticism rightly lived, the *Life of Macarius* tells us, can lead to self-emptying and profound concern and compassion for others.

The Coptic Life of Macarius and the Lausiac History

The Coptic *Life of Macarius of Alexandria* (or, as the *Life* refers to him, Macarius the Alexandrian) is fragmentary and untitled; the beginning of the codex is missing, and the *Life* begins towards the end of the story of the saint's visit to the tomb of Jannes and Jambres (*Lausiac History* 18.9). That story occupies much of the first nine paragraphs of the eighteenth chapter of the *Lausiac History* (18.5–9); since the Coptic *Life* includes its conclusion, it is reasonable to assume that the Coptic also originally contained a version of the entire beginning of chapter eighteen, paragraphs 1–9.

The Coptic *Life*, in fact, closely follows the order of the Greek *Life*; the major exception is the story of Macarius' healing of a hyena pup (par. 2), which occurs toward the end of the *Lausiac History* (18.27–28), but in the Coptic *Life* immediately follows the story of the visit to the tomb of Jannes and Jambres. The Coptic *Life*, however, includes eleven paragraphs (as numbered in the present translation) not found in the *Lausiac History*: 6, 11–14, 20–24, and 26. Paragraphs 6 and 26 seem to be doublets, but the other paragraphs offer important and interesting material about Macarius, most of it not found elsewhere: his confrontation with robbers (par. 11, with parallels in *Apophthegmata* Macarius the Great 40 and 18); Macarius' vision of the angel of the altar (par 20); the miracle of the chalice (par. 21); the visit of the mimes (par. 22); and Macarius' visit to Alexandria (par. 23).

Intriguingly, some of the additional material contradicts—or supplements—information about Macarius found elsewhere. Paragraph 4 (with a parallel in *Lausiac History* 18.10) says that Macarius "had a number of cells in the desert: he had a cell in the interior desert; he had another in the interior of Libya; he had another in the monastic community called the 'Cells' and another in the monastic community of Pernouj [Nitria]," while paragraph 14 adds that "he had three cells at Scetis: one next to the great interior desert, one situated in the middle of Scetis, and one near people, a short distance away." The editor, like an ancient redactor of the Pentateuch, has added additional information without effacing the seemingly contradictory evidence that precedes. In this case, perhaps he was trying to situate Macarius more locally in Scetis whereas the other source locates him in all three famous monastic communities of lower Egypt: Nitria, Kellia, and Scetis.[9] In par. 12 Macarius says, "From the day that I became a monk I have not eaten my fill of bread and I have not slept as much as I could." In the *Virtues of Saint Macarius* 77 this saying is attributed to Macarius the Great, while in *Praktikos* 94 Evagrius seems to be assigning it to Macarius of Alexandria.[10] Paragraph 22 declares that "they also said about Saint Abba Macarius the Alexandrian that when he was a young man living in Alexandria he was a mime by trade and was world-famous." *Lausiac History* 17.1 (Coptic *Life of Macarius the Great* 1), by contrast, says that as a young man he was "a vendor of confectionaries." Perhaps he was both. It is clear that multiple traditions were circulating about Macarius in antiquity and that in the Coptic *Life* someone placed these traditions not side by side but one after another, without seeing any disparity between them.

What is most striking about these traditions—both in the *Lausiac History* and in the Coptic *Life*—is that "anonymous" third-

---

[9]Par. 7 locates him in Scetis. Part of the contradiction in these sources is removed if "Scetis" is understood more broadly as encompassing both the Cells and Scetis (Wadi al-Natrun), an understanding that Evelyn White has recommended.

[10]Guillaumont believes, "Le problème," 51–52, that the "holy father Macarius" referred to in *Praktikos* 94 is not Macarius of Egypt but Macarius of Alexandria, despite the clear reference in *Praktikos* 93 to Macarius the Egyptian. (Guillaumont does not refer to the *Virtues*). He believes that Evagrius "generally designated" Macarius of Alexandria with the epithet "the holy father Macarius."

person narrative combines with eyewitness ("I," "we") accounts and secondary testimony ("his disciple told me," "they also said"). Roughly half of both the Coptic and Greek *Lives* claim that their material comes from primary and secondary accounts; thus there is no radical difference between the presentation of the material in the *Lausiac History* and the "extra" material in the Coptic *Life*.[11] For example, with regard to the story of Mark the Ascetic (par. 16; *LH* 18.25), in the *Lausiac History*, Palladius says that Macarius himself told him about Mark; in the Coptic *Life*, it is Macarius' "disciple who . . . still lives in the monastic community" who narrates the story. This same disciple is also the source for the "extra" material in pars. 20–21. Par. 20, an apophthegm, takes the classic form of early monastic oral tradition where "A tells B who tells C": "Abba Macarius' disciple told me, 'My father said to me, "Not a Saturday or a Sunday passed that I did not see the angel of the altar standing in front of me as I celebrated the Holy Communion of God." ' " In the *Apophthegmata*, such "linearity" lays claim to authentic tradition, to the wisdom of the old men. The same is true here. Part of par. 12 seems to have Evagrius as its source.[12] Judged solely by form and origins, then, the extra material in the Coptic *Life of Macarius of Alexandria* has as much claim to authenticity as that in the *Lausiac History*.[13] It seems possible that Palladius even wrote some of it.

[11]The Coptic *Life* may offer evidence of the omission of one eyewitness from the *Lausiac History*: Palladius says that he himself saw the sinful priest healed by Macarius (*LH* 18.19–21); the Coptic *Life* (par. 9) begins this story "Another time I was with him along with Saint Albinus." Albinus the Roman, son of Anatolius the Spaniard, is mentioned in the Coptic *Life of Pambo* 10. He apparently was a friend of Evagrius (*LH* 47.3, if this Albanius/Albinus is the same person) and may have been omitted from the Greek text of *LH* 18.19 by an anti-Evagrian editor.

[12]See *Praktikos* 94.

[13]Guillaumont, "L'Enseignement" 85–86, has shown how the *Apophthegmata* moved from first person and attributed accounts to third person, unattributed accounts. Stories told in the first person seem to point to an early stage of the tradition.

SYNOPTIC TABLE

The Coptic *Life of Macarius of Alexandria & Lausiac History* 18

Coptic *Life*	*Lausiac History*
1. Macarius Returns from the Tomb of Jannes and Jambres	*LH* 18.9
2. Macarius Heals a Hyena Pup	*LH* 18.27–28
3. Abba Macarius and the Asp	*LH* 18.10
4. Abba Macarius' Cells	*LH* 18.10
5. Abba Macarius Heals a Young Woman	*LH* 18.11
6. Abba Macarius Gives Relief to Another Young Woman	—
7. Abba Macarius Goes to Visit the Pachomians	*LH* 18.12–16
8. Abba Macarius Ascends to Heaven in His Cell	*LH* 18.17–18
9. Macarius Heals a Sinful Priest	*LH* 18.19–21
10. Abba Macarius Heals a Young Man	*LH* 18.22
11. Abba Macarius and the Robbers	—
12. A Rule Concerning Eating and Sleeping	—
13. His Meager Clothing	—
14. His Three Cells	—
15. Abba Macarius Battles and Defeats Vainglory	*LH* 18.23–24
16. Abba Macarius' Disciple Tells about Mark the Ascetic	*LH* 18.25
17. Macarius in Old Age	*LH* 18.26
18. Paphnutius Tells about Abba Macarius	*LH* 18.28
19. Abba Macarius' Appearance	*LH* 18.29
20. Abba Macarius Speaks about the Angel of the Altar	—
21. The Miracle of the Chalice	—
22. Abba Macarius and the Mimes	—
23. Abba Macarius Goes to Alexandria	—
24. Concluding Remarks	—
25. More Concluding Remarks	*LH* 18.29
26. Final Remarks	—

The *Life of Macarius of Alexandria* was read in the Coptic *Synaxary* on 6 Paschons.

[LIFE OF MACARIUS OF ALEXANDRIA]
(*LAUSIAC HISTORY 18*)[14]

Macarius Returns from Visiting the Tomb of Jannes and Jambres (LH 18.9)[15]

1   [235] [Macarius said,][16] ". . . immediately the antelope turned over and [showed] me her breasts streaming with milk. Then I knew right away that God wished to keep me alive and I heard a voice, 'Macarius, arise, go to the antelope, drink the milk, and recover your strength and go to your cell.'" He went and drank her milk and slept

[14]The beginning of the codex is missing and the codex lacks a title. Translated from E. Amélineau, *Histoire des moines de la Basse-Egypte* (Paris: Lernoux, 1894), 235–61, with corrections supplied from Vat. copt. 69 by Adalbert de Vogüé, "Le texte copte du chapitre XVIII de l'*Histoire Lausiaque*: L'édition d'Amélineau et le manuscrit," *Orientalia*, 61.4 (1992): 459–62. Numbers in brackets give the pagination of Amélineau's text. References to the Greek text of the *Lausiac History* are to G. J. M. Bartelink, ed., *Palladio: La Storia Lausiaca* (Milan: Fondazione Lorenzo Valla, 1974), which is a modification of Butler's. Translations of the Gk text are from *Palladius: The Lausiac History*, trans. Robert T. Meyer (Ancient Christian Writers 34; New York: Newman, 1964). Section titles and paragraphing are my own. Portions in italics are lacking in Gk. Paragraphs without "*LH*" in parentheses lack parallels with the *Lausiac History*. Paragraph numbers do not correspond to *LH* but are given for ease of reference.

[15]The manuscript has a lacuna at the beginning and picks up with the end of the story of the visit to the tomb of Jannes and Jambres (*LH* 18.5–9); thus the missing portion probably contained a version of *LH* 18.1–8. *Historia Monachorum* 21.5–8 (Russell, 152) makes Macarius the Great the hero of this story, while the Latin version gives that role to Macarius of Alexandria; see Guillaumont, "Le problème," 52.

[16]In Gk the story is told entirely in the third person. The Coptic soon switches from first person to third, then back to first, a fairly common occurrence in Coptic translations of Greek texts.

a little. The antelope went away and one of them, either her or another one, gave him milk each day. "And when I drew near my cell and was a day's walk from it, all the antelope went away and left me. I returned to my cell on the eighth day."[17]

Macarius Heals a Hyena Pup (LH 18.27–28)[18]

2   One time *while he was [sitting in his cell]*, a hyena came to him, *carrying her cub in her mouth.*[19] She *placed the cub in front of his door and* knocked on the door. *The old man heard her knock and came out, thinking that a brother had come to see him. When he* [236] *opened the door he saw the hyena. He was amazed and said, "What do you seek here?"* She picked up her cub with her mouth and offered it to the old man, *weeping.*[20] The old man took the cub in his hands *with his customary simplicity; he turned the cub this way and that, inspecting its body to see where it might be hurt. When he examined the cub, he discovered that it was*[21] *blind in both eyes.* He took it, *sighed,*[22] spit into its face, *and made the sign of the cross on its eyes with his finger.*[23] Immediately the cub could see *and left him for*[24] its mother and suckled. *[It followed] her and they went [into] the river there and into the marshland and disappeared.*

---

[17]Although the text here and *LH* 18.9 are clearly related, they are also quite different.

[18]Both the Greek and Coptic versions of the *Lausiac History* make Macarius of Alexandria the focus of this story while *Historia Monachorum* 21.15 has Macarius the Great; since the *Virtues of Saint Macarius* has several stories like the one here (see *Virtues* 14), such confusion is understandable.

[19]In the Gk, Paphnutius, a disciple of Macarius', tells this story.

[20]See *Virtues of Macarius* 14, where an antelope weeps. That story has a number of affinities with this one.

[21]Am: *afoi*; Vogüé: *nafoi*.

[22]Or: groaned, *affi ahom.*

[23]and made . . . finger: Gk, "and then prayed."

[24]Reading *isken* as *isjen.*

The Libyans bring their sheep to the marshland of Scetis once[25] *a year to eat herbs*[26] *and the herdsmen who live in the villages around Pernouj* [Nitria] *also lead their cattle down to the marshland of Scetis once a year to eat grass.*[27] The hyena let one day go by but the next day she came to the old man with a sheepskin, *very plush and soft, hanging from her mouth as an offering,* and knocked with her head on the door. The old man was sitting in the courtyard. When he heard [237] the knock on the door, he got up and opened the door and found the hyena holding the skin as an offering. He said to the hyena, "Where have you come from? Where did you get this unless you ate a sheep? What you have brought me has come from violence. I will not accept it from you."

The hyena was hitting her head on the ground and bending her paws,[28] *imploring him like a person to take the sheepskin from her.*[29] He said to her, "I just said that I would not accept the sheepskin unless you promise me not to hurt the poor by eating their sheep." She moved her head even more up and down, as though she were giving him her promise. Once again he repeated himself to her, saying,[30] "Unless you promise me you will not kill any living beast but will eat only carrion from now on, [I will not accept the sheepskin].[31] From now on, if you are weary from searching for food and are unable to find anything to eat, come to me here and I will give you bread, and do no violence to anyone from now on." The hyena prostrated herself to the earth, throwing herself on her knees, bending her paws, moving her head up and

---

[25]Am: *nouson*; Vogüé: *nousop.*

[26]Coptic *shoushēt,* an "herb eaten by sheep" (Crum 603B), contrasted with *ouōtouet* that the cattle eat below. BV translate it as "*l'herbe,*" while Am transliterate the word.

[27]For the ancients, from Herodotus on, the Nile separated Asia from Libya (Africa) [BV].

[28]The Coptic has alliterative play here: *kōlh . . . epkahi . . . neskeli eskōlj.*

[29]See Rufinus *EH* 2.4; Sulpicius Severus *Dialogues* 1.15; *Virtues of Saint Macarius,* Am 134–35 (= *Virtues* 14) [BV].

[30]Vogüé+: *efjō mmos.*

[31]This clause is missing from the Coptic, but seems required to complete the sense.

down, looking[32] *up into his face, as though she were giving him her promise.*

And the old man understood that it was the economy of God that gives intelligence[33] *even to wild beasts in order to teach us a lesson. And he gave glory to God* [238] *who gives intelligence even to wild beasts,*[34] *and he sang praises in Egyptian to God who exists for ever, because the soul is precious.*[35] *He said, "I give glory to you, God, who were with* Daniel in the lions' den [Dan 6:22–23][36] *and gave intelligence to wild* beasts. In the same way now you gave intelligence also to this hyena *and did not forget me but made me understand that this was your ordinance." And the old man accepted the sheepskin from her. The hyena returned to her lair again and every few days would pay him a visit. If she was unable to find food, she would come to him and he would throw bread to her. She would often do this.*

The old man slept on the sheepskin until he went to his rest.[37] *I saw it with my own eyes. Indeed, when he was about to die,* Melania,[38] *queen of the Romans, happened to pay him a visit.* He gave that sheepskin to her as an inheritance.[39] *It remained in her possession until her death; she faithfully kept it as a remembrance.*[40]

[32]Vogüé+: *esjousht.*

[33]*Kati* is used as a noun here and as a verb in "understood" immediately above.

[34]See *Virtues* 36.

[35]Or: honored, *staiēout.* Both Am and Vogüé believe that the text is corrupt.

[36]Gk: "And what is so remarkable about this, that He who subdued the lions for Daniel should also enlighten the hyena?"

[37]Am: *shatefti mton;* Vogüé: *shatefmton.*

[38]Am: "melania"; Vogüé: *melianē.*

[39]Gk: "The blessed Melania told me: 'I took that fleece as a visiting-gift.'"

[40]See *Life of Antony* 92, and *Life of Pambo* 6 where Melania receives a basket from Pambo before he dies. *Lausiac History* 18.28 and Paulinus of Nola *Letter* 29.5 confirm that Melania received the skin, while *Historia Monachorum* 21.16 says that the "skin is still in the possession of one of the brothers."

Abba Macarius and the Asp (LH *18.10*)[41]

3   Another time he dug a well in the middle of some reeds. There was an asp *sleeping there that no one knew about.* That asp *was a killer and it was hiding in the rushes on account of the cold. When the sun rose, the earth warmed up.* [239] *The old man came and stood on the earth without knowing about the asp. The asp was injured and* bit the old man on the leg. *He caught the asp alive in his hands and said to it, "What harm*[42] *have I done to you that you attempt to eat me? God has not given you authority to do this; therefore it's your evil nature to do so. I will do to you according to your own evil nature* [Gen 3:14].[43] And the old man seized the two lips of the asp in his two hands, pulled them apart, and tore it in half *down to its tail.*[44] *He left it in two pieces and in this way the old man did not suffer at all* [Acts 28:3–6] *but was like someone who has been stuck*[45] *by the point of a reed.*

Abba Macarius' Cells (LH *18.10*)

4   This Abba Macarius had a number of cells in the desert: he had a cell in the interior desert;[46] he had another in the interior of Libya; he had another in the monastic settlement[47] called the "Cells" and another in the monastic settlement of Pernouj.[48] Some of them were without doors,[49] for in truth they were located in the interior desert

[41]For a similar story, see Tim Vivian and Apostolos N. Athanassakis, trans., *The Life of Saint George of Choziba* (San Francisco: ISP, 1994), 56.

[42]Am: *piji nčons*; Vogüé: *piči nčsons*.

[43]Am: *tenmetsa mpethōou*; Vogüé: *tenmetsa nnethōou*.

[44]*Peflēs*, an uncertain word. Crum, 145a, suggests "jaw." Am and Vogüé suggest "tail."

[45]*Lōks* can also mean "bite," but is a different verb from the one used above (*lapsi*) for "bit." Gk concludes: saying, "If God did not send you, how did you dare come?"

[46]Gk: "one at Scete in the innermost part of the Great Desert."

[47]Or: mountain, *pitōou*.

[48]Gk: Mount Nitria. See below, par. 14, where it says he had three cells in Scetis.

[49]Gk: "windowless."

where he did not encounter anyone: these were where he lived during the season of Lent, *dark caves lying beneath the earth, similar to hyenas' dens*; indeed, they were so narrow that he was not able to straighten out his limbs [240] at all.[50] But the cell near to people[51] was spacious; this was where he met the brothers.

Abba Macarius Heals a Young Woman (LH 18.11)

5   This old man, Saint Abba Macariuis,[52] healed a number of people possessed by demons, so many that their numbers were countless. Thus, while we were there, a young woman[53] who was paralyzed and very sick was brought to him.[54] *When this woman heard news of him in her own land, she had herself brought to him, and after he had prayed over some oil* he anointed her *whole body many times with his holy hands.* After twenty days *God healed her* through his prayers and Abba Macarius sent her home whole, having been healed[55] *and giving glory to God. After she reached her city, at the the end of three days she died. She left three hundred pieces of gold when she went to her rest: in her will she bequeathed them to Saint Abba Macarius on account of the way she had been healed.*[56]

Abba Macarius Gives Relief to Another Young Woman

6   *The fame of Saint Abba Macarius spread and another young woman heard about him. She went to him from Thessalonica. Her*

---

[50]See Jerome *Life of Hilarion* 4.13, 21.5; Sozomen *EH* 3.14; Theodoret *History* 3.5 [BV].

[51]Gk: "another cell."

[52]Gk: "he."

[53]Or: virgin, *parthenos*. Gk: suffering from paralysis for a good many years.

[54]In Gk she is from Thessalonica; see par. 6.

[55]In Coptic, "whole" and "healed" are related etymologically: *ouoj* and *oujai.*

[56]After . . . healed: Gk, "After she had gone away, she sent him gifts of fruit."

name was Lydia; she was a scribe, copying books for reading. She prac-
ticed a strict ascetic regimen, living a man's way of life. She spent a
whole year [241] *living in a large cave. She would meet the old man*
once a day; no one else saw her in the whole monastic settlement except
on the day she left the settlement in order to return to her own country.
And her hidden thought came to the old man: through the old man God
gave her relief[57] *by means of the old man's prayers.*[58] *She returned to*
her own country, giving glory to God because he gave her relief through
her visits to the old man.

Abba Macarius Goes to Tabennesi to Visit the Pachomians (LH 18.12–16) [59]

7   This Macarius heard one time that the men of Tabennesi *(which
is a monastery in Upper Egypt)* performed a number of ascetic practices because they were very great men. Abba Macarius rose, changed
his clothes, and put on peasant's clothing as though he were a work-
man. He went to Upper Egypt, walking through the desert fifteen
days until he arrived there.[60] When he reached the great monastery,[61]
he went and sought the father[62] of the monastery whose name was
Abba Pachomius. He was someone chosen and proven and he possessed the gift[63] of prophecy. God told him nothing concerning

[57] *Ti mton* means "to give rest, relief," and can indicate relief from an illness.

[58] Text: *nentōbh,* "our prayers," which, followed by *mpikhello,* "of the old man," is
a mistake.

[59] *AP* Macarius of Alexandria 2 confirms that Macarius visited the Pachomians,
but the *apophthegm* it gives bears no relation to the much longer story here. A
shorter version of this story, attributed to Macarius the Great, seems to occur in the Coptic
Sayings of Macarius of Egypt 26 (see the companion volume to this one, *Saint Macarius the Spiritbearer*).

[60] It seems very unlikely that Macarius would have walked to Tabennesi; it is more
likely that he would have made his way to the Nile, then taken a boat upstream to the
Pachomians.

[61] Gk: "Arriving at the monastery of Tabennesi."

[62] Correcting *phmōit* to *phiōt* with Am and Vogüé. Gk: "archimandrite."

[63] *Hmot* also means "grace."

Abba Macarius; to be sure, he had heard about him and wanted to see him.[64] When Abba Macarius met Abba Pachomius, he said to him, "I implore you, my father, receive me into your [242] monastery.[65] Perhaps I too might become a monk."

Abba Pachomius said to him, "*What do you want, my brother? See here, looking at you and judging by your age,* I see that you are an old man. You will not be able to live a monastic way of life, and all the brothers here are ascetics. You will not be able to endure their stringent practices and you will have your feelings hurt; you will leave speaking evil of the brothers. *Go to the hospice for visitors and workers and stay there. I will see that you are fed there until you want to leave on your own.*"

He received him neither on the first day nor the second, not until the seventh day.[66] When Abba Macarius became weak from persevering in not eating, he *again went to meet the leader of the monastery and* said to him, "Receive me *into your monastery, my* father, and if I am unable to fast *and practice asceticism* and work with my hands like the others, drive me from your monastery." Then Abba Pachomius sent to the brothers to take him inside. The number of brothers there was 1,400 monks in the monastery.[67]

Abba Macarius went and when he had spent a few days there, the time came for the holy forty days of fasting[68] and he saw all the brothers doing various ascetic practices, some one thing [243] and some another: some were fasting until evening each day while others were fasting two days and others five days; still others were fasting while standing all night and sitting during the day. Abba Macarius

[64]Gk: "This latter did not know Macarius."

[65]Gk, *monē* here; earlier in the par. Coptic *abēt* is used.

[66]The Rule of the Four Fathers calls for the same delay. Cassian, *Institutes* 4.3.1. and 4.36.2, says ten days or longer, while Pachomius, *Precepts* 49, leaves the waiting period unspecified [BV].

[67]*LH* 32.8 gives a figure of 1,300; Jerome, *Praef. in Regula Pachomii* 2, supplies a figure of between 1200 and 1600 per monastery and in *Praef. in Regula Pachomii* 7 gives a total of 5,000 for the entire Pachomian *koinonia*. Cassian, *Institutes* 4.1, says there were more than 5,000 [BV].

[68]That is, Lent.

went and soaked his palm branches in water, *took them, placed them in a round*[69] *seat elevated in front of him*. He stood in a corner of his cell *plaiting palm branches* until the forty days were over. *He did not sit at all, nor did* he eat bread or drink water, nor did he bend his knees,[70] but each Sunday he would take some cabbage leaves and eat them in front of the brothers so they would know that he was eating. And if he went outside to urinate or to soak some palm branches, he hastily fled inside at once. He did not speak with anyone nor did he open his mouth at all but stood in silence, praying in his heart while working with the palm branches.

When all the ascetics saw what he was doing, they rose up against their leader of the monastery, saying, "Where have you brought this old man from? Maybe he's not even flesh and blood! Have you brought him here in order to judge us? Either you throw him out of the monastery or all of us will leave!" When Abba Pachomius heard about the kind of ascetic practices Abba Macarius was doing, he prayed to God to reveal [244] to him the truth about the old man and who he was.

God revealed to him *that this was Abba Macarius the Alexandrian who lived in Scetis.*[71] And *the leader of the monastery* took the old man's hand and led him into the midst of the area where they hold the synaxis *after they finish the eucharistic prayer in the sanctuary*[72] so that the whole crowd of brothers might see him, and he said to him, "Come here, venerable sir.[73] Are you Abba Macarius?[74] You have hidden yourself from us. How long I have heard about you and have

---

[69]Text: *outots nkurikon*, which Am translates "*une table ronde* (?)." As Vogüé points out, 137 n. 23, this translation supposes correcting *-kuri[a]kon* to *-kyklikon*, which Am does not do. BV translate "un support rond," but do not exclude the possibility that *kurikon* is correct.

[70]Gk +, "or lie down."

[71]Macarius of Alexandria was a priest at Kellia, or the Cells, so either he is mistaken here for Macarius of Egypt or "Scetis" includes Kellia.

[72]Literally: "the prayer of the place where they perform the sacrifice." That is, the altar or the sanctuary; the prayer (singular in the MS. but plural in Am's text) is the eucharistic liturgy [BV]. Gk is simpler: "into the oratory where the altar was."

[73]Coptic/Gk: *kalogēros*, which means "monk" in modern Greek.

[74]Gk is a statement.

wished to see you! But I give thanks to you because you have edified all of us[75] and have taught the young brothers not to be vain about their ascetic practices. *Even if they do everything, they can not match the forty days of our Lord and Savior Jesus Christ, Son of the living God* [Mt 16:16]. *Especially since, although you seem to be a man like us, you have done all these ascetic practices as an old man.* Go home *in peace*; you have edified all of us sufficiently.[76] And pray for us." Then he left *as all of them did obeisance to him and beseeched him, "Pray for us."*

Abba Macarius Ascends to Heaven in His Cell (LH 18.17–18)

8   He also told us this other story: "Every ascetic practice that I had undertaken [245] I had successfully completed, but the desire also entered my heart to do this: I wanted to spend five days with my heart focused on God at all times without paying any attention at all to the ways of this age. Having made this promise in my heart, I entered my cell *in the interior desert, the one without door or window or any light,*[77] so no one could find me, and I stood *on the mat in my cell.*[78] I fought with my thought,[79] speaking thus: '*Watch yourself.* Do not come down from heaven: there you have the patriarchs and prophets and apostles; there you have the angels and archangels and the powers on high *and the cherubim and seraphim. Cleave to God: the Father and the only-begotten Son and the Holy Spirit, the consubstantial Trinity, God of gods* [Ps 50:1], *the king of all the ages* [1 Tim 1:17].[80] *Climb high upon the cross of the Son who*[81] *is in heaven.* Do not come down from that mighty[82] place.'[83]

[75]Gk: "my children"; see *Life of Antony* 82, 91.
[76]Gk: "for you have stayed long enough with us."
[77]Gk: "I shut up my cell and the hall."
[78]Gk: "at the second hour."
[79]Gk: "I gave these orders to my mind."
[80]Gk: "the God of all of us."
[81]Or: "which."
[82]Or: "victorious," *-jor.*
[83]Gk: "heaven."

"And when I had finished two days," he said, "and two nights, the demons became so demented that *they changed themselves into a crowd of phantasms. Sometimes they took on the appearance of lions scratching my feet with their claws;*[84] *sometimes* [246] *they took on the appearance of serpents entwining themselves around my feet. Finally,* they took on the appearance of fiery flames in order to burn up everything inside the cell, even the mat I was standing on; they burned up everything except for the soles of my feet so that I thought I too was going to be burned up. Finally, the fire and the phantasms fled.[85] *On the fifth day* I was unable to master my thought without distraction *but I returned to worldly worries and human ways of seeing. I understood that if I was going to succeed in completing this commandment, I would destroy my understanding and become insanely arrogant.*[86] For this reason I was at peace allowing the cares of this world into my heart so I would not fall into arrogance." *He added words like these: "I have spent fifty years doing ascetic practices without suffering anything like I did that day."*

Macarius Heals a Sinful Priest (LH 18.19–21)

9   Another time I was with him *along with Saint Albinus.*[87] A village priest came to Abba Macarius; his whole head was peeled away because he was consumed by the disease called "cancer," which had eaten away his whole face, and his head was so peeled away that when you looked at it you saw no flesh but only bone. [247] *He was very horrible to look at. The priest had lost everything he had on doctors and had not been healed* [Mk 5:26, Lk 8:43]. *When he had lost hope* he went to the old man so that God with him might heal him of his illness. *Therefore he threw himself down at the old man's feet and implored*

---

[84]See *Life of Antony* 9.6–7, 52.2.
[85]Gk: "Finally, overwhelmed by fear, I left on the third day."
[86]Thus insane (*-libi*), he would become like the demented (*libi*) demons.
[87]On Albinus, see n. 11 above.

him, but the old man completely ignored him.[88] We[89] implored him, however, saying, "Our father, have pity on this man. *Don't ignore him.* Answer him in his distress."

And he said,[90] "*Let him be;* he doesn't deserve to be healed. If he had stopped fornicating he would still be going up to the altar."[91]

The priest spent three days imploring him, but the old man ignored him. Finally, he took pity on his tears and his supplication; he called him and said to him, "Do you know why God has brought this chastisement upon you?"[92]

He answered him, "Yes, *my lord.*"

Abba Macarius said to him, "Have you been able to mock him?" [Gal 6:7]

He said, "No, *my lord.*"

The old man said to him, "Since you have acknowledged your sins, if you turn away from them you will be saved."

Then the priest confessed his sin. The old man said to him, "Why have you not given up your priestly position in order not to be cast into eternal punishments and be saved?"

[248] *Then we said to him, "Wretch,[93] promise the old man that you will not go up to the altar so God may heal you through the prayers of this saint."*

And when he had promised the old man "I will not go up to the altar," and when the old man had prayed over oil, he anointed his entire head and face and God gave him healing.[94] His head grew skin

[88]Literally "turned his face completely away from him." In Coptic, "to beg, beseech, implore" is *ti ho,* while "ignore" is *kōti mpefho sabol.* Both employ *ho,* "face."

[89]Gk: "I."

[90]Gk adds: "to me."

[91]Literally: "the place of sacrifice," the altar, a phrase used later in the *Life.* Even though the priest had stopped fornicating, he was continuing to function sacerdotally, a transgression in Macarius' eyes. The Gk is longer here.

[92]Gk: "When I told the afflicted man this, he agreed, and he vowed that he would no longer exercise the priestly function. Then Macarius received him, saying, 'Do you believe that God exists?' "

[93]Literally, "weak one." *Jōb* can indicate physical or moral weakness or, as here, both.

[94]Gk: "And so Macarius laid his hand on him, and in a few days he was cured."

again and hair.[95] The old man dismissed him and he went away, saying, "I will remain a lay person until I die."[96]

Abba Macarius Heals a Young Man Possessed by a Demon
(LH 18.22)

10   This other event took place when we were present: A young man possessed by a demon[97] was brought to him. The old man placed one hand on his head and his other hand he placed over the young man's heart. *His heart aflame,* he prayed to God *for an hour* without ceasing so that the demon was suspended high in the air, *crying out and saying, "Have pity on me!"* The young man became like a wineskin, so swollen was his body, and when he spoke in a loud voice, his eyes and ears and nose and mouth and all his lower members[98] *gushed like water pouring from a bottle*[99] and when he poured out all the water he returned to normal. *Then the old man held the young man in his arms as he prayed and said,* [249] *"Glory to you, Lord Jesus Christ, who saves those who have faith in you!"*[100] And he poured[101] a pot[102] of water over him and anointed him with holy oil, *while he gave him a little water to drink.* And he commanded him: "Do not eat meat for forty days and do not drink wine" [Rom 14:21]. And when he was healed, the old man gave him to his father, healed.

---

[95]Am: *phōi*; Vogüé: *fōi*.
[96]Gk: "he went away cured."
[97]Gk: "evil spirit."
[98]his eyes . . . members: Gk, "all his sense organs."
[99]See Jerome *Life of Hilarion* 8.8 [BV].
[100]Vogüé+: *erof.* The Coptic switches from "you" (*nak*) to "him" (*erof*).
[101]Am: *jōf*; Vogüé: *jōsh.*
[102]Am: *noubalkon* (for *balkou*); Vogüé: *noulakon* (= Gk *lakanē*).

Abba Macarius and the Robbers[103]

11   *Again one time there was a famine over the whole earth and among the Libyans who lived on that mountain; as a result, some Libyan robbers came searching the desert one time.*[104] *They came upon the cell of Abba Macarius with a camel in their possession, having loaded waterskins on it with water to drink in the desert. When they entered the cell of Abba Macarius, they found nothing of value in his cell. They seized all the bodily necessities and his handiwork and a few palms and took them and loaded them on the camel.*

Now it happened that when they had loaded the bags on the camel and wanted to get it up, the camel was unable to get up; it was bellowing but was unable to get up. Then morning came. All of a sudden the old man returned. He saw [250] *the men and the camel from a distance and thought that they had brought him some bodily necessities from Egypt in order to receive his handiwork from him in return, as was his custom.*[105] *But when he got closer to them, he recognized his baskets and his palms and his few bodily necessities. He kept quiet and said nothing.*

When they saw the holy old man, they prostrated themselves and made obeisance to him and begged his forgiveness over and over. He, however, did not get angry nor did he beat them but walked right by them, went into his cell, and found that[106] *they had taken all his possessions in the cell except for a small pot, which had a few olives in it. (They had not seen it sitting behind the door.) The old man, the good old man,*[107] *picked up the pot of olives, took it outside to them, and said to them, "Do you want to know why the camel was not able to get up?"*

They said, "Yes."

He said to them, "Because you forgot these few olives; that's why you've been unable to get the camel up." And after he placed the pot on

---

[103]For a similar story, see *AP Macarius the Great* 40 and 18.

[104]V+: *nousop.*

[105]See *Life of Antony* 53.1.

[106]Vogüé says that the text reads *de* instead of Am's *je*, but the sense requires *je.*

[107]*Nkalokērōs*; see above, par 7 n. 73.

the camel and gave the animal a kick, it immediately got up. And he sent them away in peace and accompanied them off.[108]

The next day some brothers came to see the old man, having traveled to hear some profitable words from him. It was already time to eat [251] and the brothers wanted to eat a little something. Therefore, when he knew their thoughts, he said to them, "There's bread in your traveling skins; bring it here so we can eat a little something, for God has given the bodily necessities that were here in my dwelling to some men of the world who have wives because some poor folk needed them due to the severity of the famine."

A Rule Concerning Eating and Sleeping

12   He also said this other saying in the presence of the young brothers in order to prompt their emulation: "From the day that I became a monk I have not eaten my fill of bread and I have not slept as much as I could.[109] None of the mighty fathers were ever sick, because they would direct their bodies by a well-regulated rule."

His Meager Clothing

13   He told us this other saying concerning himself: When he was young,[110] he spent an entire year without putting on any clothing except for an old rag wrapped around his loins and his members.

---

[108]*AP* Macarius 40 ends here.

[109]In *Praktikos* 94 (Bamberger, trans., 40), Evagrius attributes a similar saying to "the holy Father Macarius." Bunge, "Évagre le Pontique et les deux Macaires," 221–22, 223, regards this Macarius as Macarius of Alexandria. *Virtues* 78 attributes it to Macarius of Egypt.

[110]Am: *nsēou*; V: *psēou*.

His Three Cells

14   *He had three cells at Scetis: one next to the great interior desert, one situated in the middle of Scetis, and one near people, a short distance away.*[111]

Abba Macarius Battles and Defeats Vainglory (LH 18.23–24)

15   Another time the thought of vainglory *and pride* afflicted Abba Macarius, wanting to drive him from his cell.[112] [252] *The thoughts would say to him, "Macarius! Your name has become famous throughout the whole world. Get up!* Go to Rome, *the city of kings,*[113] *so you can heal those who are sick*[114] *and not afflict them by making them come all this distance. Indeed, the Romans are united with the Egyptians with regard to their ascetic practices and their orthodox faith."*[115] *With this pretext, then, the demons wanted to drive him from his cell. They would say to him, "God has put this inclination in your heart along with a great gift*[116] *for healing. Get up, go, for this is God's dispensation."*[117]

When he saw that they afflicted him,[118] he sat at the threshold of his cell[119] and said to them, "If you can, take me from here by force." *Once again, when the demons afflicted him by laying difficulties upon him,* he cried out with a loud voice and with anger,[120] "I've already

[111]See above, par. 4.

[112]In this sentence the thought (*pimeui*) is singular while the participle (*euouōsh*) is plural; in the next sentence the thoughts (*nimeui*) are plural.

[113]Gk: "to promote the designs of Providence."

[114]Gk adds: "for grace against spirits worked strongly in him."

[115]Either this was written before the Council of Chalcedon (451) or it is meant ironically, that the declaration of such a union is a pretext of the demons.

[116]Also: grace, *hmot.*

[117]*Oikonomia.*

[118]Gk: "And as he did not take heed for a while, but was strongly pressed."

[119]Gk adds: "put his feet outside."

[120]Gk: "he declared an oath."

told you that I don't have feet;[121] if you are able, pick me up and carry me to Rome. Look! I will sit here until the sun sets."

After he sat there a while, he got up, and when night fell the thoughts[122] afflicted him again and he took hold of a basket and put two measures of sand in it.[123] He hoisted it up on himself and walked around with it throughout the desert. And he came upon [253] Theosebeia the sweeper.[124] He said to Abba Macarius, "What are you carrying there, *my* father? Set it on me. Do not afflict yourself."[125]

Abba Macarius said to him, "I am afflicting that which afflicts me,[126] for truly, if I give it rest, it brings thoughts to me, saying, 'Get up! Go to the stranger.'"[127] After he continued walking around in the desert,[128] he returned to his cell, his body crushed.

Abba Macarius' Disciple Tells about Mark the Ascetic (LH 18.25)

16   *His disciple who served him in his old age*[129]—*to whom he entrusted the duke's son because he was a believer who came to live with the old man and who still lives in the monastic community working with his hands, eating by means of his labor* [2 Thess 3:10], *very hospitable to strangers*—*this faithful disciple of Abba Macarius, then, told me, "My father Abba*[130] *Macarius told me,*[131] 'I saw at the time of the mysteries

[121]Gk: "O demons, I shall not go on my feet."

[122]Gk: "the demons"; Evagrius often uses "demons" and "thoughts" interchangeably.

[123]See *Life of Pachomius* (SBo 10 = G1 6) [BV]; Armand Veilleux, ed., *Pachomian Koinonia* (Kalamazoo: Cistercian, 1980), 1.33.

[124]*Pikosmitēs* (Gk *kosmētor*); see Lampe 769B under both. At Scetis an Abba Paul was known as Paulos *ho kosmitēs*; he and his brother Timothy were *kosmitai* [BV]. Gk: Theosebius the Sweeper, he of Antioch born.

[125]Am: *mperti khisi*; Vogüé: *mpefti khisi*, but the former seems required.

[126]See *LH* 2.2 [BV]. Gk: "I am molesting my tempter."

[127]Gk: "he is uncontrollable and tries to throw me out."

[128]Gk adds: "for a long time."

[129]See *Life of Antony* 91.1.

[130]Am lacks; Vogüé+.

[131]Gk: "This holy Macarius told me this also, for he was a priest."

that I did not give the sacrament[132] to Mark the Ascetic a single time but when he came to receive communion I would see an angel placing the sacrament in his hands.' "[133] *Abba Macarius was priest of the church while* Mark himself was a young man who had learned the Old and New Testaments by heart. He was a very gentle person and chaste.

Macarius in Old Age (LH 18.26)

17   One day, then, when Abba Macarius was an old man, I went [254] to pay him a visit.[134] I sat by the door so I could hear what he said. Abba Macarius had reached a hundred years. I heard him talking all by himself, saying, "What do you want, Macarius, you wicked old man?[135] Look now, you drink wine and use oil; what more do you want, you who have eaten your own gray hair?"[136]

After this he spoke with the Devil, "Have you nothing more to do with me? There's nothing for you here. Get away from me!"[137]

He acted as though he despised his body, speaking like this: "Go away, traitorous horse! You will never be well as long as I am with you!"[138]

Paphnutius Tells about Abba Macarius (LH 18.28)

18   Another time Paphnutius, the disciple of Abba Macarius,[139] told us, "The old man said to me, 'Look, it's been seven years today since I recall spitting on the ground.' "[140]

[132]Literally "give blessing," *ti smou*; see Crum, 336A.

[133]Gk adds: "I saw only the wrist of the minister's hands."

[134]The beginning of this story in Gk is considerably longer.

[135]-*kakogeros* contrasts with *kalogeros* earlier; see pars 7 n. 73 and 11 n. 107.

[136]The Gk is clearer: "you gray-haired old glutton."

[137]See Sulpicius Severus *Epistle* 3.16 [BV].

[138]Gk: "And, as though humming, he kept saying to himself: 'Come, you white-haired old glutton, *how long shall I be with you?*' "

[139]In the *Virtues of Saint Macarius* and *Life of Macarius of Scetis*, a Paphnutius is the disciple of Macarius of Egypt.

[140]In the Gk (*LH* 18.27), Paphnutius first tells the story of the hyena (par. 2

Abba Macarius' Appearance (LH 18.29)

19   Abba Macarius had the appearance of a dwarf,[141] with a few hairs growing above his lips and on the end of his chin.[142]

Abba Macarius Speaks about the Angel of the Altar

20   *Abba Macarius' disciple told me, "My father said to me, 'Not a Saturday or a Sunday passed that I did not see the angel of the altar*[143] *standing in front of me as I celebrated the Holy Communion of* [255] *God.' "*

The Miracle of the Chalice

21   *Yet again I heard another very amazing story from him*[144] *when he said: "I was present on one of the feast days when the deacon was inside the sanctuary preparing the eucharistic offering.*[145] *The chalice fell from his hand and broke into numerous pieces, for it was glass (truly, it was the desert and it was not possible for them to have silver). I myself heard the sound of the chalice breaking when it fell from the deacon's hand. I entered the sanctuary while all the people*[146] *were seated saying the psalms. I said to the deacon, 'Don't be upset and don't*

above), then in 18.28 it is Macarius who says that "from the time he was baptized he did not spit on the ground, and it was then sixty years since he had been baptized," clearly an independent *apophthegm* that has been appended to 18.28.

[141]Gk: *hypokolobon*; Coptic: *-kolobos*. John "the Little" (also called "John the Dwarf") is John Kolobos.

[142]Gk continues: "for the asceticism he practiced did not allow hair to sprout on him." *LH* 18.29 then appends what seems to be a separate *apophthegm*.

[143]Or: sanctuary; literally, "the place of sacrifice," as seen above and in the next par.

[144]The disciple is apparently speaking.

[145]Literally: "gift," *dōron*.

[146]*-laos*.

get discouraged, but gather up all the pieces and do not leave any behind. Put them on the altar, go, and leave them.' And when Saint Abba Macarius left, he and the deacon, they sat a short while.[147] *Abba Macarius said to the deacon, 'Go to the altar. Tell no one what you are going to see there.' The deacon went inside and found the chalice in perfect condition: it was put back together. The signs of the broken fragments were visible, but it no longer looked dropped. That chalice still exists today.*

"*When I heard about this miracle, I went to the deacon, who had become a priest.* [256] *He showed me that chalice. I saw it with my own eyes. I kissed it and glorified God. When the father of the monastery of Tashenthosh*[148] *of the village of Jani*[149] *came, he paid a visit to the monastic community. He brought a large supply of money*[150] *and distributed it to the old men of the desert places.*[151] *He asked the priest there for that chalice and the priest gave it to him as a token of remembrance. Indeed, that chalice resides in the monastery of Tashenthosh to this very day.*"

Abba Macarius and the Mimes

22   *They also said about Saint Abba Macarius the Alexandrian that when he was a young man living in Alexandria he was a mime by trade and was world-famous.*[152] *When he had become a monk, exalted in*

[147]Abba Macarius and the deacon possibly were saying the Psalms with the people.

[148]A monastery in the eastern Nile delta; see Wolfgang Kosack, *Historisches Kartenwerk Ägyptens* (Bonn: Rudolf Habelt, 1971), 90, and in that volume, "Karte des koptischen Ägypten" 6C (grid number).

[149]Sa el-Hagar; Kosack, 35 (under Jani), and "Karte" 6C (grid number).

[150]*Diakonia*; see Lampe 351A (A2).

[151]This is the first time that the plural, "deserts," has been used; perhaps it indicates the various monastic communities or the various old men scattered throughout the desert. It occurs in the next paragraph, where it perhaps suggests the several settlements where Macarius lived.

[152]Literally: great in the world. "World" might be pejorative here. The theme of "the world" will appear again later in the par. See *LH* 17.1 (Coptic *Life of Macarius the Great* 1), where Macarius of Alexandria is "a vendor of confectionaries."

virtue in the desert places, his fellow mimes heard that he had become exalted in God's work [Jn 6:29, 1 Cor 15:58]. They came to see him in the desert, seven in number, and when they had greeted him they sat beside him. They were full of admiration for him and his way of life. When it came time for them to eat, he put water in the pot and carried it to the oven, wanting to cook some cereal for them. While he heated the water to bring it to a boil, before he poured[153] the meal into the pot he sat and chatted with them as he had when he had been a mime[154] living in the world.

When they saw [257] how he was behaving, they said to one another, "Weren't we told that he had become a man of God? Now look—he's the same as he was when he was in the world with us. We don't see any change from the way he behaved when he was with us in Alexandria."

When Abba Macarius saw them speaking with one another about the great freedom of speech he used with them, he brought in an empty dish, gave it to the greatest among them, and said to him, "Fill this dish with sand and pour it into the pot so we can cook the cereal and eat."

When they heard "sand," they joked among themselves, saying, "Truly Macarius has become more of a mime now than when he was with us in the world!"

Once again he said to them, "Do what I told him."

They obeyed him: they filled the plate with sand and poured it into the pot. He made the cereal and it turned out like a cereal made from tasty wheat. When the seven mimes saw the miracle that had taken place through the holy old man Abba Macarius, they did not return to Egypt but renounced the world. They became monks and adopted the practices of the holy old man Abba Macarius.

[153] Am: *mpatefi*; Vogüé: *mpatefhi*.
[154] Am: *mmos*; Vogüé: *mmimos*.

Abba Macarius Goes to Alexandria

23   [258] *They also told this concerning the righteous Abba Macarius the Alexandrian: One time the sky would not rain on the earth and multitudes of worms and pests[155] appeared in the people's fields. Abba Timothy, archbishop of Alexandria,[156] sent some envoys to Abba Macarius to beseech him: "Come to Alexandria. Entreat God to cause it to rain and kill the worms and pests."[157]*

When they persuaded him with great entreaties, he went with them to Alexandria, When he drew near the city, a great crowd came out to meet him with palm branches [Jn 12:13]. When he reached the Tetrapylōn, which is in the middle of the city, he prayed to God with all his heart.[158] When he came to the Gate of the Sun,[159] the sky began to pour forth drops. When he entered the church, it rained heavily for two days and two nights without interruption;[160] as a result, the people thought that the earth would be inundated and overwhelmed by the large amount of rain in the air.

The old man said to the archbishop, "For what purpose have you sent for me? Why have you caused me to forsake my cell and come here?"

---

[155]*Chansrōf* (cf. *kōns*?); Crum 516B, "name of a field pest?" Am: insectes; BV: sauterelles.

[156]Archbishop from 381–85.

[157]Am: *nichonsrōf*; V: *nichansrōf*.

[158]The Tetrapylon, attested only in Christian sources from late antiquity, was evidently an arched structure, located in the center of the city. No trace of it remains. See Christopher Haas, *Alexandria in Late Antiquity: Topography and Social Conflict* (Johns Hopkins, 1997), 193 and 368, note 27. The city of Aphrodisias had a 16-columned tetrapylon.

[159]The "Gate of the Sun" was the eastern gate of the walled city. No trace of that remains either, but the location can be established with some degree of certainty. See Haas, *Alexandria*, 30, 31 and 211. The Gate of the Sun was "guarded" by the Sun divinity. Evidently most travelers to Alexandria from Egypt entered through the Gate of the Sun, which was built by Antoninus Pius (138–161) and marked the formal boundary of the fortified city. The Sun Gate stood near a quarter filled with hostels and accommodations for travelers and also functioned, not surprisingly, as the "red light" district. A church was established by the gate dedicated to Saint Metras, an Alexandrian martyr who was dragged out of the city and stoned during the reign of Decius.

[160]See Jerome *Life of Hilarion* 22.4 [BV].

The crowds [259] *answered him, "We brought you here to have you pray for it to rain—and now look, you have taken pity on us! This downpour is enough! Pray, therefore, for the rain to depart from us, lest it destroy all of us*[161] *and we all die, we and our children and our livestock and everything that we own!"*

The holy old man Abba Macarius prayed, and immediately the rain slackened; at the same time, the sky cleared through the grace of God and the prayers of Saint Abba Macarius. Then the pagans of Alexandria cried out, saying, "A magician[162] *enters the Gate of the Sun and the judge did not know about it!"*

Abba Macarius spent three days there. He healed a multitude of people with illnesses there, some of them paralytics, and a multitude of other kinds of illnesses in the three days that he spent in Alexandria when he came there from the desert.[163] *This came about through God in order that a multitude might be saved and that he might give the gift*[164] *of rain through Saint Abba Macarius.*

After these events, he left Alexandria and returned again to Scetis with the power of God. The brothers said to him, "Our father, did you go to Alexandria?"

He said to them, [260] *"Believe me, my brothers, neither column nor city center did I see; neither one. Nor did I see the face of any person except for the archbishop's alone. Crowds of people mobbed me unmercifully, surrounding me, but I decided not to lift my eyes up to anyone on earth in order to give my eyes no occasion for sin."*[165]

---

[161]Am; codex: *tērou*, "everything."

[162]See Jerome *Life of Hilarion* 11.12 [BV].

[163]For Antony's healing of people during his second visit to Alexandria, see *Life of Antony* 69–71.

[164]*Hmot* also means "grace."

[165]See *AP* Isidore 8. After a trip to Babylon, John the Little has the same words for his disciples, teaching them at greater length about pride; see Maged S. Mikhail and Tim Vivian, trans., "Life of Saint John the Little," *Coptic Church Review* 18.1–2 (1997): 3–64, at 50.

Concluding Remarks

24 *I will stop now concerning the works of Abba Macarius. Thus,
then, was the truly perfect and mighty Abba Macarius, a person*[166] *who
was worthy to be beloved. He was gentle like Moses* [Num 12:3]. *Being
very zealous, he made the young zealous to stand in virtue, saying to
them, "I have never relaxed my labors in asceticism." He was worthy of
being beloved by everyone, being very compassionate. Moreover, they
say about him that he practiced every virtue that he saw, and those that
he heard about too.*[167]

More Concluding Remarks (LH 18.29)

25 *I wanted, then, beloved, to tell you many things about Abba
Macarius, but these I have been able to relate will have to suffice.* These
are just a very few of his ascetic practices and ways of life.

    *He was a perfect old man. The day of his perfection, when he went
to his rest, was the sixth of Pashons.*[168]

Final Remarks

26 [261] *Let this suffice concerning the marvellous works of Saint
Abba Macarius the Alexandrian. We have let this suffice lest the work
become too voluminous. These things that we have spoken are sufficient
and will profit those who hear them and do them so they may obtain
the portion and inheritance of this truly mighty Abba Macarius of
Alexandria—or, rather, Abba Macarius of the heavenly Jerusalem, the
city of all those who rejoice in the grace and mercy and love for humanity of our Lord and Savior Jesus Christ* [Titus 2:4], *to whom be the glory
for ever and ever. Amen.*

[166]Vogüé+: *pirōmi.*
[167]See *LH* 18.1–2.
[168]May 1.

Seven Goals of Anti-Origenism

According to Gabriel Bunge and Adalbert de Vogüé, the *Lausiac History* was not only written "in the spirit of Evagrius," but also devoted much of its attention to Evagrius and his friends, a fact that was systematically suppressed, and thus is little in evidence in the published Greek text. The author of the *Lausiac History* was a well-known representative of Origenism and a disciple of Evagrius and Ammonius, the latter of whom was the veritable leader of the Origenist party. With the condemnation of Origenism in 553, a work like the *Lausiac History*, written "in the spirit of Evagrius" and giving a large part to Origenist monks, had to pose serious problems to monastic communities that had delighted in it up to that time. The measures taken—most likely in Palestine—closely resembled the attitude adopted towards the writings of Evagrius. These writings could not be totally suppressed, but they could not be copied and read as before.[1] The works that were least obviously Origenist were passed on under the name of Saint Nilus, under whose guise monks could

---

[1]Bunge has pointed out, "Évagre le Pontique et les deux Macaires," 352–53, that of the seven apophthegms in the *textus receptus* of the *Apophthegmata Patrum* (probably edited in Palestine), only one, Evagrius 7, is really an apophthegm; the others are extracts from Evagrius' works—but only from the ascetical writings. Recent scholarship has added two other sayings but these three sayings present a "decapitated" understanding of Evagrius' ascesis (354). The Tall Brothers are omitted entirely from the *Apophthegmata Patrum*. A comparison of the Greek and Latin texts of the systematic collection of the *Apophthegmata* shows that Evagrius' name was systematically excluded by later editors; see Gk I.4 (Latin I.4), Gk I. 5 (Latin I.5), and Gk III.2 and 5 (Latin III.3).

continue to read them as before. The work of Palladius, by contrast, suffered severe expurgation for the purpose of suppressing the memory of the Origenist monks and the contacts that Palladius had had with them. What emerged was a "neutral" *Lausiac History* and a Palladius who, in a certain sense, was another person. Although quite visible, the suppression was not imposed throughout the *Lausiac History*, and the continual contamination of the manuscripts by each other has fortunately preserved in good part that which had initially been so assiduously eliminated.[2] Here are seven "goals" of anti-Origenism as presented by Bunge and Vogüé:

1. To eliminate all connection between Palladius and the "Origenists": Evagrius (with exceptions; see #6), Ammonius or one of his brothers, certain persons susceptible of Origenism, a monk named Origen, Albinus, and sometimes even Melania the Elder.

2. To eliminate the connections between Pambo and the "Tall Brothers." Pambo's steward seems to have suffered the same fate solely because of his name (which we see happening also in the Coptic *Life of Pambo*)![3]

3. To remove the connection between Evagrius and the two Macarii, attested by Evagrius himself, Socrates, Rufinus, Gennadius, the Coptic *Lives* of Macarius the Great and Evagrius and the *Virtues* of Saint Macarius. There is no trace of this connection in the *Lausiac History* and the *Apophthegmata*.

4. To systematically expurgate the *Life of Ammonius*. His connection with Evagrius, well-attested elsewhere, is truncated; his brothers are not mentioned, nor his death in exile.

5. In order to erase all memory of Origen and other great Alexandrian thinkers, their names have been suppressed or replaced with ones more orthodox.

---

[2]BV 77–78.

[3]For similar editorial decisions made to the mss. of the *Historia Monachorum*, see Bammel, "Problems of the *Historia Monachorum*," 100.

6. Evagrius' name is suppressed throughout. An apparent exception is *Lausiac History* 35 where the connection between Evagrius and Palladius is not suppressed, but this is probably due to the continuous contamination between the different manuscript traditions.[4]

7. The censure of Origenism is not limited to these: in numerous manuscripts the *Life of Evagrius* (*Lausiac History* 38) is completely missing. The oldest complete Greek manuscript of G gives *Lausiac History* 38 as an appendix.

[4]On the treatment of Evagrius in the *Historia Monachorum*, see Bammel, "Problems of the *Historia Monachorum*," 100.

Syriac *Lausiac History* [72] and [73][1]

TRANSLATED BY ROWAN A. GREER

In *Lausiac History* 47, "blessed Evagrius" and Albanius and Palladius visit Chronius and Paphnutius. The recent deaths of some monks and the moral fall of others prompt the question, answered by Paphnutius, of why some ascetics living in the desert end up deceived by their own thoughts or wrecked by lust, and what is God's role in all this.[2] The five who had moral falls were Stephen, Eucarpius, Heron of Alexandria, Valens of Palestine, and Ptolemy the Egyptian in Scetis. The stories of Heron (*LH* 26), Valens (*LH* 25), and Ptolemy (*LH* 27) are told elsewhere in the *Lausiac History*, but those of Stephen and Eucarpius are not. The Syriac version of the *Lausiac History*, however, preserves two chapters that appear, in the words of one scholar, to "have their roots in concrete experiences which troubled the monastic life not only at Cells but also at Scete" and seem to have been written by Palladius.[3] If these chapters are authentic, they offer more evidence that the received text of the *Lausiac History*

---

[1]Translated from René Draguet, ed. and trans., *Les formes syriaques de la matière de l'Histoire Lausiaque* (CSCO 389–90, 398–99, Scriptores Syri 169–70, 173–74; Louvain: Secrétariat du Corpus SCO, 1978), Syriac text: 2.2 [398, 173]: 368–72.

[2]On this subject, see Jeremy Driscoll, "Evagrius and Paphnutius on the causes for abandonment by God," *Studia Monastica* 39.2 (1997): 259–86.

[3]Driscoll, "Evagrius and Paphnutius," 270. On their authenticity, see Draguet, 173:365, and Gabriel Bunge in BV 53–55, 68–69, 76–80. Driscoll, "Evagrius and Paphnutius," 266–67, says that the Syriac chapters "certainly appear to be from the hand of Palladius."

was altered in transmission, and thus give support to the suggestion that the Coptic versions of the same work may preserve better, less truncated, readings. One notes also the prominence of "blessed Evagrius" in both chapters (72.3, 73.4), a possible reason for the later ellision of these texts.

CHAPTER [72]
STEPHEN

1   There was a man at Scetis whose name was Stephen. He had lived in the desert twenty-nine years and was clothed with netting. He so conducted himself in humility and abstinence that he did not allow himself to take any satisfaction at all in anything desirable or that held pleasure. He strongly criticized those who ate cooked meat or drank wine except because of sickness. He had been given the gift of healing so that he drove out demons by a word. Once a man with an unclean spirit came to Scetis and asked to be healed. When [Stephen] saw that the man was harshly tormented by the demon, he uttered a prayer over him and healed him. Afterwards [Stephen] was deprived of divine care because of a measureless pride and lofty self-esteem. He thought himself better than the other abbas because of his ascetical observances.

2   First of all he separated himself from the brotherhood and became abbot of one of the monasteries on the outskirts of Alexandria. For he said in his lofty self-esteem, "I am in slavery under Macarius. Are not my ascetical observances better than his?" He went so far in his insanity that he entered Alexandria and became accustomed to profligacy, drunkenness, and to eating meat beyond the order observed by rational people. Finally, he fell and wallowed in the pit of lust for women, constantly making the rounds of the houses of prostitution and the innkeepers' taverns. He was joined with prostitutes, and he shamelessly and lasciviously fulfilled his lust for them so that he became a laughing-stock to all who knew him.

He gave an excuse to all who knew him by saying, "To the perfect no law is given." And he said, "I am not doing this through passion," and "there is nothing to hate in fornication; there is no longer sin in it, since male and female were created by God."

3   One day I and blessed Evagrius went to Alexandria, summoned by a particular purpose. There were four brothers with us. When we were crossing one of the city's market places, [Stephen] met us by accident while he was speaking with a prostitute because of his obscene lust. When blessed Evagrius saw him, he wept, fell at his feet, and prostrated himself. But [Stephen] did not bow his head even a little. Instead, in pride and lofty self-esteem without limit he answered and said, "What are hypocrites and deceivers looking for here?" Blessed Evagrius implored him to go with us to our lodgings, but he was absolutely unwilling. Nevertheless, when with difficulty he consented to go with us, after we went in and prayed, blessed Evagrius fell on his neck, kissing him and weeping. And he said to him, "Truly, my beloved, from such a lofty service of the angels you have lowered yourself to such a pit of evils; from conversation with God you have turned to conversation with prostitutes; instead of the service and ministry of angels you have chosen the service of demons. Yet even if Satan has been able to cause you to fall so badly, nevertheless I ask and implore you not to abandon hope of your salvation. Instead, get up and come with us to the desert; and by the hands of the merciful God it will happen that he will return you to your former rank." But [Stephen] was so blinded in his mind by Satan that he did not understand how to hear anything that was said to him, nor did he give any answer. He said to Evagrius, "Up till now I have been wandering far afield, but now I have found the truth." He broke out mocking the abbas and said, "You are the ones wandering far afield. It is by outward clothing that you dwell in the desert because of human beings and not because of God. For those who see you, you are like idols that people love and adore." And so, filled with pride and Satan's boasting, he despised the abbas and left to go away. Blessed Evagrius and all the brothers wept and groaned over him greatly.

4   Now [Stephen] brought to his monastery for a corrupt purpose a virgin who was an orphan, a hermit, and an ascetic—as though she would be near him to help with their alms, but really to fulfill his lust. Now after he had been in his lapsed state for the space of about two years, at last brigands came upon him at night. They bound him and beat him harshly and painfully until he brought out everything he had in the monastery and laid it before them. Last of all they shut him up in a house where there was straw—him and the woman with whom he fulfilled his lust, both of them bound. They set fire to the house. Both of them were burned and died a painful death. And so what was said by the teacher of the Gentiles was fulfilled upon them: "Because they have not judged it right in themselves to know God, God has handed them over to the knowledge of vanity and of degrading their bodies among themselves, receiving in themselves the penalty that was justly due" [Rom 1:28, 1:24] for their fornication, namely the burning with fire here below, the pledge of that fire which will torment all the wicked.

5   All these misfortunes happened to Stephen because he separated himself from the brotherhood, became proud in his mind, and thought that he was perfect.

Chapter [73]
Eucarpios

1   There was also in the desert a man named Eucarpios. He had spent eighteen years shut up in a cell, while others took care to supply his wants. He kept silent for fifteen years without speaking to anyone at all. But if he needed anything, he wrote on a piece of paper and gave it to those who served him. He did the same thing when someone asked his opinion or spoke with him. His food consisted of beans soaked in water and preserved vegetables. He labored in this way of life beyond measure. He, too, was finally mocked by the demons because of their vain opinion of him.

2   First of all, he separated himself from communion and association with the brothers and from meditation on the Holy Scriptures;
and he devoted himself entirely to constant prayer. And so he exalted
himself, became proud in spirit, and supposed that he had become
perfect and that, as a consequence, he saw God continually in his
spirit because of his purity of heart.

3   The Tempter, then, also tempted him [1 Thess 3:5] just as he had
blessed Job. One night Satan appeared to him in the form of an angel
of light and said to him: "It is I who am the Christ" [2 Cor 11:14].
Eucarpios, then, when he saw him, thought that the vision was true.
He fell down, worshipped him, and said to him: "What does my Lord
command his servant?" The one who appeared to him said to him:
"Because you have excelled many by your disciplines and have kept
all my commandments, I have desired to make my abode with you
[Jn 14:23]. But now that you have been perfected it is no longer necessary for you to shut yourself up, nor is it right that you should keep
silent. Rather, you should teach all the brothers not to busy themselves with reading the Scriptures and with the office of the Psalms,
not to toil with bodily labors, not to wear themselves out with
hunger, thirst, and fasting. Instead, teach them to toil with the labors
of the soul so that they may quickly be able to ascend to the highest
rank and constantly behold me in their minds, and I will show them
my glory [Jn 17:24]. As for you, because you have been exalted above
all of them, today I appoint you chief and commander over all the
hermits who live in Scetis. Macarius is not as suitable as you are to
be the leader." Eucarpios, then, exalted himself still more and
became proud in spirit. He was convinced and believed in the
Deceiver's lie, for his reason was taken away from him; and his mind
was deranged as soon as he worshipped the Adversary.

4   It happened that the next day there was an assembly in the
church, and Satan appeared to Eucarpios a second time and said to
him: "Come, today all the brothers are assembled. Teach them everything I commanded you last night." And so Eucarpios opened the
door of his hermitage and left to go to the church. Now it happened

that Abba John was sitting beside the church, and the brothers were gathered round him questioning him about their thoughts.[4] When Eucarpios came and saw John and the brothers around him, he was filled with jealousy against him. He spoke up and said to John with pride and evil anger: "Why do you adorn yourself and sit like a harlot to multiply your lovers? Or who has commanded you to direct the brothers, while I am the leader?" When the brothers heard this, they were disturbed and said to him: "Who has made you the leader in Scetis?" Eucarpios said to them: "It is I, last night, I who have been made leader by Christ. From now on turn to me, and I will teach you the path by which you may easily ascend to the highest rank of the glorious vision. Therefore, do not stray after Evagrius' writings, nor listen to John's words. You have strayed in them long enough until now." And he began to revile the fathers. He called Macarius an ornamented idol that those who had strayed worshipped, since he did not know how to lead the brothers to heavenly things. He called Evagrius a sculptor of words, causing the brothers to stray after his writings and stopping them from spiritual exercise. And so he was mocked by the demons so that they lifted him up and hurled him down to earth. Now it was in all this that Eucarpios fell: because he reviled and despised the brothers through his pride and boasting and because he was unwilling to meditate on the Holy Scriptures and the teaching of the fathers.

5   After all this when the fathers saw that he was deranged in his mind, they put him in irons and bound him. And while keeping him in irons, the holy fathers offered prayers for him at all times for eleven months. His understanding returned to him, and so he was healed of his pride and recognized his weakness. The saying was fulfilled for him, "old wounds are healed by cauterization," and "you who have been exalted to heaven shall be brought down to Sheol" [Ps 107:26]. Now after he had been healed from his pride, he lived a year and one month. The fathers commanded him to minister to the sick and to wash the feet of strangers. And so he died.

[4]This apparently refers to John the Little; see *AP* John Kolobos 46 and Mikhail and Vivian, "Life of Saint John the Little," 26.

Evagrius Debates Three Demons
(*LH* 38.11)

Lausiac History 38.11 gives a very terse account of an encounter between Evagrius and three demons: "Three demons disguised as clerics attacked him in broad daylight and they examined him as regards the faith; one said he was an Arian, one an Eunomian, and the third said he was an Apollinarian. He got around them with his knowledge and a few words" (Meyer, 113–14). This story is intrinsically interesting, but the account here is so brief that it is difficult to glean much from it. The Coptic *Life of Evagrius* 29 offers a much expanded version of the confrontation, one which makes the version in the *Lausiac History* look like a condensation. A Greek fragment of the event, though shorter than the Coptic account, confirms this: at some point Palladius must have written a longer version of this story.

Dom Cuthbert Butler decided that the Greek fragment is the original, because its "minute heresiological knowledge seems more akin to the acute Greek mind than to the Coptic, which appears not to have been versed in metaphysical speculation."[1] Scholars are less prone now to dismiss Coptic theology, but Butler is undoubtedly right that the account was originally written in Greek—which leads to the intriguing questions: When did Palladius write it? And why did it get abbreviated almost to nothing in the *Lausiac History*? Once again we are probably confronted with anti-Origenist tendencies

---

[1]Butler, 1.135.

that sought to downplay the role of Evagrius in the *History*. Whatever may be the case, the longer Greek and Coptic fragments supply us with a fascinating story from early monasticism, one that, had we the *Lausiac History* alone, would pass by almost unnoticed.

FROM THE LIFE OF THE HOLY[2] EVAGRIUS WRITTEN BY PALLADIUS

Greek (Cotelerius/Butler)[3]

Three demons in the form of clergy[4] met him during the middle of the day.

Their idea[5] (to disguise themselves) was so good that he had no idea they were demons. Indeed, his door to the courtyard was always kept barred; when he found it shut, he knew immediately that his visitors were demons.

Each, therefore, asked him his own question, and they said to him, "Since we have heard that you speak articulately concerning the faith, we

Coptic Life of Evagrius[6]

Once again, three demons in the form of servants of the Church came to see him one day in the heat of midday, and they were dressed in such a way that they were able to prevent him from recognizing that they were demons. On account of this, after they had left and he found the door closed, he realized that they were demons, but he did not realize it at first. They had given the appearance of discussing with him the subject of faith in the scriptures, and each of them told him his concern and they said to him, "We have heard it said that you speak articulately about the orthodox faith; therefore,

[2]Or: saint, *hagiou.*

[3]Translated from the text edited by J.-B. Cotelerius, *Ecclesiae graecae monumenta III* (Paris, 1686), reproduced from Paris Gk 1220 f. 271v by Butler, 1.132–35.

[4]Or: dressed as clergy, *en schemati klērikōn.*

[5]Text: *euphuesanta*, which is unattested, probably a denominative verb from *euphuia.*

[6]Translated from the text edited by É. Amélineau, *De Historia Lausica, quaenam*

have come so you might persuade us."

He said to them, "Say what you wish."

The first said, "I am a Eunomian; I came in order for you to tell me: Is the Father unbegotten or begotten?"

He said to him, "I will not answer you, for you have not asked a good question. With regard to the begetting of the Unbegotten, no one can use the term 'begotten' or 'unbegotten.'"

Thus left at a loss, he brought forward the other one. When he came, he brushed aside the one who went before him because he had asked a bad question.

So Abba Evagrius asked him, "Who are you?"

"I," he said, "am an Arian."

"And what do you want?"

"With regard to the Holy Spirit," he said, "and with regard to the body of Christ, I want to know if Mary truly bore it."[7]

we have come to you so you might satisfy our concerns."

He said to them, "Ask what you wish."

The first said to him, "I am a Eunomian. I have come to you so you might tell me whether the Father is begotten or unbegotten."

Apa Evagrius said to him, "I will not answer you because you have asked a bad question, for it is not right to talk about the nature of the Unbegotten and to inquire whether it is begotten or unbegotten."

When the first realized that Evagrius had defeated him, he pushed his companion forward. When he had come forward, he first said [to his companion] "You've put your question badly."

Apa Evagrius said to him, "And you, who are you?"

He said, "I am an Arian."

Apa Evagrius said to him, "And you in turn, what do you seek?"

He said to him, "I am asking about the Holy Spirit and about the body of Christ, whether or not it was truly him whom Mary bore."

---

sit huius ad Monachorum Aegyptiorum historiam scribendam utilitas (Paris, 1887): 121–24, with important corrections by Adalbert de Vogüé, based on Vatican Copt. 64, "Les fragments coptes de l'Histoire Lausiaque: l'édition d'Amélineau et le manuscrit," *Orientalia*, 58.3 (1989): 326–32.

[7]Literally: if truly this [refering to "body"] is of/from Mary.

Abba Evagrius answered, "The Holy Spirit is neither something begotten nor a creature, for every creature is circumscribed by place and is subject to change and is sanctified by participation in the divine.

But the Holy Spirit proceeds from the Father[8] and fills all things[9]—I mean things in heaven and things on earth. It is sanctified by no one. Therefore, what is uncircumscribed[10] and immutable and holy by essence can neither be a creature nor be called one. With regard to the body, the question is one asked by Manichees and Valentinians and Marcionites. Do the Arians also ask it?"

The demon replied, "Yes, we have our doubts, but we do not dare express them publicly on account of the rabble."

Abba Evagrius responded, "Numerous events and statements demonstrate that his body was from Mary: growth and circumcision, and nine months gestation in the womb, and breastfeeding, and eating and drinking, and suffering,[11] and sleep

Saint Evagrius said to him, "The Holy Spirit is neither an offspring nor a creature. All creatures are limited in place. All creatures are subject to change and are sanctified by him who is better than they."

[8]See Jn 15:26.

[9]Sg 1:7.

[10]Or: the uncircumscribed (Holy Spirit). The neuter might be generic or might be refering to the Holy Spirit, which is gramatically neuter. Evagrius uses a different term here (*aperigrapton*) for "(un)circumscribed" than earlier (*periorizetai*).

[11]Or: weariness, *kopos.*

belong to the corruptible body;[12] even more striking was when he was on the cross and was stabbed by the lance and poured forth blood and water."[13]

Thus when the second was also left at a loss, the third came forward with great boldness, pushing aside the other two because they had gained no advantage[14] over Abba Evagrius, and said to him, "I grant that you have prevailed over these two; to be sure, the truth was on your side. What do you have to say to me?"

Evagrius said to him, "What do you doubt?"

He responded, "I don't have any doubts; I am certain that Christ did not have a human mind[15] but instead of a mind had God himself: a human mind can not defeat the Prince of Demons."[16]

[The third one said,] "You have defeated these two, for some [. . .] will you wish to speak to me too?"

The old man said to [him], "What do you seek, you who pride yourself in doing battle?"

The demon said to him, "Me? I'm not arguing with anyone, but my mind is not persuaded or certain that Christ received human intelligence. Rather, in place of intellect God himself was in him. Indeed, it is impossible for human intelligence to cast out the Prince of Demons from human beings and defeat him. Indeed, human intelligence can not exist in the body with God."

[12]See Lk 2:21, Lk 2:52, Mt 8:24, Jn 4:6.

[13]See Jn 19:34.

[14]Reading *aprokopous* with BV and Cotelierus instead of *aproskopous* with Butler. In M.Gr. *prokopē* means "getting somewhere, having substance," while *aprokopos* means "ineffective."

[15]"Mind," *nous*, has also been translated below as "intellect," "intelligence."

[16]See Mt 12:24.

He said to him, "If he did not have human intelligence, he did not have a human body either,

and one could say that he was not called Christ.[17]

Paul, when he sums up the faith in unity, teaches the fact of immutability *and* about *both* the human soul *and* the body: 'For there is one God and one mediator between God and humankind: Christ Jesus, human.'[18]

Apa Evagrius said to him, "If he did not receive human intelligence, he did not receive human flesh either. If, therefore, [he] received human flesh from [Mary the] holy Virgin, then [he] also [became] human, with a soul [and intellect], being complete in everything except sin alone. For it is impossible for the body to exist [without receiving] a soul and intellect. If, therefore, he did not receive these, then he is called Christ in vain. Therefore, the unchangeable Logos, the only-begotten Son of the Father, received a human body and soul and intellect and everything human except sin.

Let it suffice us, therefore, at present to offer solely the apostle Paul as witness, who, bringing together the faith in a single unity, speaks of a single divinity and a single royalty: the consubstantial and unchanging Trinity. 'For,' he says, 'one is God, one is the mediator between God and humankind, Jesus Christ,'[19] the Son of God the Father, with the one Holy Spirit, one baptism, one Catholic Church, one resurrection of the dead at the time of [. . .] as [Paul has

[17]The text is corrupt here; I have followed BV.
[18]1 Tim 2:5
[19]1 Tim 2:5.

As I see it, the three of you are in complete agreement in denying the mystery of the Holy Trinity. Since one of you says that the Word is a creature, while another rejects the Holy Spirit and the body of Christ, and ‹another›[20] the soul, it is clear that you find yourselves in agreement with the Jews who crucified Christ. They, perhaps, may be pardoned, having killed according to the flesh, but you, through your impiety, have killed him just as thoroughly according to the spirit."

Very upset, they threatened to make a public example of him, and then they disappeared. But he, as though waking from some sort of sleep, became very fearful. Therefore he sent a message to Albinus,[21] his neighbor, who was very gentle, with whom he was very close, and informed him of the incident. Albinus advised him not to remain alone, because his spirit was overly alert and because he was weighed down by solitude.

said] [. . .][22] you (pl.) deny the full mystery of the Holy Trinity. One of you has made the Logos a creature, another has made the Holy Spirit a creature and [denied] the body of Christ, and another has killed the soul and body of Christ [. . .]"[23]

---

[20] Adding ‹*ho de*› with Butler.
[21] Albinus of Rome; see *LH* 26.2 and 47.3 where he is called "the blessed Albinus" and is a companion of Evagrius.
[22] See perhaps 1 Cor 15:12.
[23] The Coptic text breaks off here.

Apa Aphou and Archbishop Theophilus Debate the Image of God

Aphou was bishop of Pemje (Oxyrhynchus), a city situated on the west bank of the Nile halfway between Heracleopolis and Antinoë; according to the author of the *Historia Monachorum*, the majority of its inhabitants were monks.[1] One saying is attributed to Aphou in the *Alphabetical Apophthegmata Patrum*; it confirms that he was bishop of Oxyrhynchus and reports that when he was a monk he led a very severe way of life.[2] The fragment translated below begins somewhere in the middle of what appears to be a *Life of Aphou* with the statement that while Aphou "was still living with the wild beasts [as an anchorite], he left for the proclamation of holy Easter," that is, for the reading of the annual festal letter of the archbishop of Alexandria in which the archbishop announced the date of Easter and the beginning of Lent and took the opportunity to instruct his flock on theological matters.[3] This opening sentence both says that Aphou had been a monk and sets the stage for his meeting with Theophilus, archbishop of Alexandria. The context soon makes it clear that the event that precipitated the meeting between monk and

[1] *Historia Monachorum in Aegypto* 5; *The Lives of the Desert Fathers*, trans. Norman Russell (Kalamazoo: Cistercian, 1980), 67.

[2] PG 65.133.

[3] On the letters, see Alberto Camplani, *Le lettere festali di Atanasio di Alessandria: Studio storico-critico* (Rome: C.I.M., 1989) and, for a partial translation, W. Cureton, ed., *The Festal Letters of Athanasius* (London, 1848). Camplani is preparing a new critical edition.

bishop was the reading of Theophilus' festal letter of 399 condemn-
ing Anthropomorphism (see the General Introduction to this volume).
Aphou hears a statement in the letter that "did not accord with his
understanding of the Holy Spirit" and, prompted by an angel of the
Lord, journeys to Alexandria to confront and correct Theophilus.

Georges Florovsky has summarized the theological issue at
stake:

> Aphou took exception to one particular expression . . . in the
> epistle of Theophilus. In his conversation with the Arch-
> bishop he was concerned solely with the concept of God's
> image in man. He did not develop or defend any "Anthro-
> pomorphite" thesis. The sting of his argument was directed
> against the denial of God's image *in man*, and there was no
> word whatever about any "human form" *in God*. Aphou only
> contended that man, even in his present condition and in
> spite of all his misery and destitution, had to be regarded still
> as being created in the image of God, and must be, for that
> reason, respected. Aphou was primarily concerned with
> man's dignity and honor. Theophilus, on the other hand, was
> embarrassed by man's misery and depravity.[4]

The fragment published below is apparently part of a hagiographical *Life of Aphou*;[5] it was preserved in Sahidic Coptic

[4]Georges Florovsky, "Theophilus of Alexandria and Apa Aphou of Pemdje," in
Harry Austryn Wolfson Jubilee Volume (Jerusalem: American Academy for Jewish
Research 1965), 275–310, repr. in Georges Florovsky, *Collected Works*, vol. 4, *Aspects of
Church History* (Belmont, MA: Nordland, 1975), 97–129, at 119.

[5]The text, from a papyrus in the Egyptian Museum in Turin, was published twice
in the nineteenth century, then early in the twentieth century by Etienne Drioton, "La
Discussion d'un moine anthropomorphite audien avec le Patriarche Théophile
d'Alexandrie en l'année 399," *Revue de l'Orient Chrétien*, 2nd series 10 (20).1 (1915–17):
92–100, and 10 (20).2: 113–28. Drioton does not give a date for the manuscript but
Florovsky, "Theophilus of Alexandria and Apa Aphou of Pemdje," suggests the seventh century and adds, 101, that "it seems most probable" that the collection of which
it is a part "was completed in the later part of the fifth century."

undoubtedly because of its opposition to Theophilus' condemnation of Anthropomorphism.[6]

APA APHOU AND ARCHBISHOP THEOPHILUS DEBATE THE IMAGE OF GOD[7]

[5] While he was still living with the wild beasts[8] he left for the proclamation[9] of holy Easter. He heard a statement that did not accord with his understanding of the Holy Spirit. As a result, he was very upset at what he heard. Indeed, everyone who heard it was saddened and upset over it. But the angel of the Lord commanded [6] blessed Aphou not to be indifferent to what was read, saying to him, "You have been appointed by the Lord to go to Alexandria to take issue with what was said." The wording of that proclamation went like this: in exalting the glory of God in the proclamation, it emphasized human weakness, and the person who had dictated it said that "this weakness is not the image of God," understanding "this weakness" to be we who bear the image, that is, we human beings.

When blessed Aphou heard these things, he was filled [7] with the Holy Spirit and departed for the city of Alexandria, wearing an old tunic. Blessed Apa Aphou stood at the bishop's door for three days and no one let him in, looking on him as though he were a bumpkin. After a while, one of the clergy took notice of him; he saw his patience and perceived that he was a man of God, so he went

[6]For further discussion, see Florovsky, "Theophilus of Alexandria and Apa Aphou of Pemdje," and Aloys Grillmeier, in collaboration with Theresia Hainthaler, *Christ in Christian Tradition* 2.4 (Engl. ed., London: Mowbray, 1996), 223–28.

[7]Translated from the text edited by Drioton, 95–100, 114–15. Numbers in bracket indicate page numbers of the manuscript.

[8]For a discussion of Aphou's *xeniteia* or ascetic wandering, see Florovsky, 101–107, and, for a more wide-ranging discussion, Daniel Caner, *Wandering, Begging Monks: Spiritual Authority and the Promotion of Monasticism in Late Antiquity* (Berkeley: University of California Press, 2002).

[9]Drioton translates: "festal letter."

inside and informed the archbishop: "Sir, there is a poor man outside the door who is saying 'I wish to meet with you,' but we have not
dared bring him to you since he is not wearing suitable clothing." All
of a sudden, as though he had been [8] prompted by God, the archbishop ordered Aphou to be brought in to him. When Aphou stood
before him, the archbishop asked him the reason for his visit. Aphou
responded: "May my Lord Bishop hear the word of his servant with
charity and forbearance."

The archbishop said to him, "Speak."

Blessed Apa Aphou responded, "I know the Christian nature of
your soul, for you are a person who accepts counsel. Therefore, I
have approached Your Greatness, confident that you will not look
down on what is said out of godliness, even if it comes from a poor
person such as myself."

Archbishop Theophilus said to him, "What godless person
would be foolish enough [9] to reject under any circumstances a
word from God!"

Aphou replied, "May my Lord Bishop order the proclamation
read to me here at once. I heard a statement in it that is not in accord
with the scriptures of the Breath of God.[10] I do not believe that it
came from you. No, I said, no doubt the scribes erred while writing
it. Many devout people were scandalized on account of this statement and as a result were greatly grieved over it."

Immediately Apa Theophilus the Archbishop ordered the
proclamation to be brought in at once. When the person began to
read the proclamation [10], he soon came to the statement in question. Immediately Apa Aphou prostrated himself and said, "Such a
statement is not right. No, I will confess that all people have been created in the image of God."

The archbishop replied, "Why is it that only you have spoken
against this statement and no one else has spoken in agreement with
you?"

[10]Drioton translates: "of the Holy Spirit."

Apa Aphou said, "I am confident that you will agree with me and will no longer oppose me."

The archbishop said, "How can you say that an Ethiopian is the image of God, or a leper, or someone who is lame or blind?"

Blessed Apa Aphou replied, "If you proclaim things of this sort you will [11] oppose him who said, 'Let us create humankind according to our likeness and image' " [Gen 1:26].

The archbishop responded, "Heaven forbid! I think that only Adam was created according to God's likeness and image. The children that Adam engendered after himself do not have the likeness of God."

Apa Aphou replied, "After God fulfilled his covenant with Noah after the deluge, he said to him, 'Whoever sheds human blood will have his own blood shed in return, for human beings have been created in the image of God' " [Gen 9:6].

The archbishop said, "I am afraid to say that a human being, subject to illness [12] and suffering, bears the image of God, who is passionless and simple. Since human beings live in society and produce things, how will you conceive of the true Light that no one can approach?"

Aphou said to him, "But if you say this, then it will be said that the body of Christ that we receive is not really the body of Christ, for the Jews will say, 'How is it that you take bread that the earth has produced and has been cultivated with hard work, and afterwards you believe that what you receive is the body of the Lord?' "

The archbishop said to him, "It is not like this. It is truly bread that we offer on the altar: when we offer it on the altar [13] and call[11] God down upon them,[12] the bread becomes the body of Christ and the wine in the chalice becomes blood, just as he said to his disciples, 'Take and eat. This is my body and blood' [Mt 26:26–28], and we believe this to be true."

---

[11]Gk/Coptic -*epikalei*, as in the eucharistic *epiklesis*.
[12]The plural seems to suggest loaves of bread or the eucharistic elements.

Apa Aphou said to him, "Just as it is necessary to believe this, it is also necessary to believe his authority: 'humankind has been created [according to] the likeness and image of God,' for he who said, 'I am the bread that has come down from heaven' [Jn 6:21] is also the one who said, 'Whoever sheds human blood will have his blood shed in return, for human beings have been created in the image of God.' With regard to the glory and majesty of God, [14] which it is impossible for anyone to see on account of his [incomprehensible light][13] and on account of human weakness and failing brought about by our natural inferiority, which we know so well, we believe this: just as a king orders his image to be painted and everyone acknowledges that it is the image of the king, at the same time everyone knows that it is wood and painted colors, for the nose on the king's painted image does not stand out in relief like a human nose, nor are the ears like those on the king's face, nor does it speak like he does. But even with all the faults that the image possesses, let no one say such things out loud, fearful of the king's opinion, for he has said, 'This is my [15] image.' What is more, if someone dares to deny that this is the image of the king, he is put to death because he has blasphemed the king. Even more, those in authority gather around the painting, praising pieces of wood and paint out of fear of the king.

"If, therefore, such things are true of an image that has no spirit and no movement, because it is antithetical to movement,[14] how much truer is it for a human being, who possesses the spirit of God, who is capable of action, and who is more glorious than all living creatures upon the earth? With regard to the different maladies and appearances[15] and weaknesses inherent in us, they are imposed on us for our salvation, for it is impossible for any of these to denigrate the glory that God has given us, as [16] Paul says, 'For the husband must not cover his head' " [1 Cor 11:4].

[13]Text: *pefou[oein] natt[ahof]*, from text edited by von Lemm (see Drioton, 92 n. 1).
[14]Text: *na[nti]thetos [n]pik[im]*.
[15]Coptic *auan* also means "color," and might be referring back to the earlier use of "colors" in the painted image, although a different word is used there.

When the blessed archbishop heard these words, he arose and prostrated himself and bowed his neck[16] and said, "Truly it is fitting for teaching to come solely from those who live in solitude; as for us, the thoughts of our hearts disturb us and as a result out of ignorance cause us to err so completely like this." And immediately he wrote to the whole country, repudiating that statement: "It errs and we believed it without thinking."

Afterwards, the archbishop adjured blessed Aphou, saying, "Tell me, what is your way of life? [17] Where are you from and who are your family? I see that your appearance is that of a peasant, but on the other hand I can hear that your words are more elevated than the words of those who are wise."[17]

Aphou responded, "I have wished to live as a monk, but I am far from that honor. I am from Pemje.[18] Since your wisdom is our foundation, the Enemy has attempted to work through you, knowing that a multitude will be stumble because of you. Therefore, they will be hurt and will not obey the word of holy instruction that comes from your mouth. But because of the love that you have for God, you defeated every kind [18] of trick played by the Devil when you listened to the words of your most unworthy servant. For even the majesty that you possess is unable to raise you up over arrogant presumptuousness so that you have control over your own will, but you have demonstrated the childlike humility that Christ possessed and the great Moses, too, when he obeyed Jethro, the priest of Midian [Ex 4:18]. Truly it was the Savior who said to our fathers the apostles, 'If you change and become like children' [Mt 18:3]. You have truly demonstrated that you have turned yourself completely away from arrogance towards the purity and simplicity of being like a child."

---

[16]Literally: "he prostrated himself upon his neck," which Drioton renders as "*se prosterna sur le front*." But one wonders if *ejm pefmakh* (neck) should be *ejm pkah* (the ground).

[17]Like Antony the Great; see *Life of Antony* 72–80.

[18]Oxyrhynchus.

Afterwards, the archbishop asked Aphou to remain with him a few days, but he [19] excused himself, saying, "It is not possible for me to stay," and so he departed from the archbishop with peace and honor. But the archbishop's heart was saddened when Aphou left him, like a child when his father leaves him.

Scripture Index

9:3	ME6	**2 Corinthians**		**1 Timothy**	
11:1–44	ME6	5:10	ME6	1:17	MA8
11:44	ME6 (2)	12:2	E24	2:5	E29
12:13	MA23			4:7	E2
		Galatians			
Acts		4:8	ME6	**Titus**	
28:3–6	MA3	6:7	MA9	2:4	MA26
Romans		**Philippians**		**Hebrews**	
7:13	E2	1:23	ME6	4:15	E29, ME6
14:10	ME6			(2)	
14:21	MA10	**1 Thessalonians**		5:14	E28
		4:5	ME6	12:14	E25
1 Corinthians					
15:44	ME6	**2 Thessalonians**		**James**	
15:53	ME6	3:8	P8	1:27	P16
15:58	MA22	3:10	MA16		

Index of Names and Subjects

Bibliography

Amélineau, É. *De Historia Lausica, quaenam sit huius ad Monachorum Aegyptiorum historiam scribendam utilitas.* Paris, 1887.

————. *Histoire des monastères de la Basse-Égypte.* Annales du Musée Guimet, 25; Paris: Leroux, 1894.

Athanasius. *Life of Antony,* ed. G. J. M. Bartelink, *Vie d'Antoine.* SC 400; Paris: Cerf, 1994.

Bammel, C. P. "Problems of the *Historia Monachorum.*" *Journal of Theological Studies,* N.S. 47.1 (1996): 92–104.

Bareille, G. "Hiéracas," *Dictionnaire de spiritualité catholique,* 6. 2359–61.

Bartelink, G. J. M., ed. *Palladio: La Storia Lausiaca.* Milan: Fondazione Lorenzo Valla, 1974.

Basil of Caesarea. *Saint Basil: The Letters,* trans. Roy J. Deferrari. Cambridge Mass.: Harvard University Press, 1950.

Bell, David N., trans. *The Life of Shenoute by Besa.* Kalamazoo: Cistercian, 1983.

Bouyer, Louis. *The Spirituality of the New Testament and the Fathers,* Vol. 1: *A History of Christian Spirituality.* Minneapolis: The Seabury Press, 1963.

Brakke, David. *Athanasius and the Politics of Asceticism.* Oxford: Clarendon, 1995.

Brown, Peter. *The Making of Late Antiquity.* Cambridge, MA: Cambridge University Press, 1978.

————. "The Rise and Function of the Holy Man in Late Antiquity." *Journal of Roman Studies,* 61 (1971): 80–101. Reprinted in Brown, *Society and the Holy in Late Antiquity,* 103–52. Berkeley: University of California Press, 1982.

————. "The Saint as Exemplar in Late Antiquity," in John Stratton Hawley, ed., *Saints and Virtues.* Berkeley: University of California Press, 1987.

————. "The Rise and Function of the Holy Man in Late Antiquity: 1971–1997." *Journal of Early Christian Studies* 6.3 (1998): 353–376.

Bunge, Gabriel. *Evagrios Pontikos: Briefe aus der Wüste.* Trier, 1986.

_____. "Évagre le Pontique et les deux Macaires." *Irénikon* 56 (1983): 215–27, 323–60.

_____. " 'Priez sans cesse': aux origines de la prière hésychaste." *Studia Monastica* 30 (1988): 7–16.

_____, and Adalbert de Vogüé, *Quatre ermites égyptiens: D'après les fragments coptes de l'Histoire Lausiaque.* Spiritualite Orientale 60; Begrolles-en-Mauges: Bellefontaine, 1994.

Burton-Christie, Douglas. *The Word in the Desert: Scripture and the Quest for Holiness in Early Christian Monasticism.* New York and Oxford: Oxford University Press, 1993.

Cassian, John. *The Conferences,* trans. Boniface Ramsey. Ancient Christian Writers 57. New York: Paulist, 1997.

Chaîne, M. "La double recension de l'Histoire Lausique dans la version copte." *Revue de l'orient Chrétien* 25 (1925–1926): 232–75.

Clark, Elizabeth A. *The Origenist Controversy: The Cultural Construction of an Early Christian Debate.* Princeton: Princeton University Press, 1992.

Coquin, René-Georges. "L'évolution de la vie monastique." *Dossiers Histoire et Archéologie* [*Chrétiens d'Egypte au 4e siècle: Saint Antoine et les moines du désert*] 133 (December 1988): 60–65.

Cotelerius (Cotelier), J.-B. *Ecclesiae graecae monumenta* III. Paris, 1686.

Crum, W.E. *Coptic Ostraca from the Collections of the Egypt Exploration Fund, the Cairo Museum and Others.* London: Egypt Exploration Fund, 1902.

_____. *A Coptic Dictionary.* Oxford: Clarendon, 1939.

Daley, Brian E. *The Hope of the Early Church: A Handbook of Patristic Eschatology.* Cambridge: Cambridge University Press, 1991.

_____. *On the Dormition of Mary: Early Patristic Homilies.* Crestwood, N.Y.: St Vladimir's Seminary Press, 1998.

_____. "What did 'Origenism' Mean in the Sixth Century?" in *Origeniana Sexta,* ed. Gilles Dorival and Alain Le Boulleuc, 627–38. Leuven: Peeters, 1995.

Daniélou, Jean. "Les démons de l'air dans la Vie d'Antoine," in Basilius Steidle, ed., *Antonius Magnus Eremita, 356–1956: Studia ad Antiquum Monachismum Spectantia,* 136–147. Studia Anselmiana, 38; Rome: Herder, 1956.

Descoeudres, Georges. "L'architecture des ermitages et des sanctuaires," in *Les Kellia: Ermitages coptes en Basse-Egypte*, 33–55. Geneva: Musée d'art et d'histoire, 1990.

Draguet, René. "L'Histoire Lausiaque, une oeuvre écrite dans l'esprit d'Évagre." *Revue d'Histoire Ecclésiastique* 41 (1946): 321–364; 42 (1947): 5–49.

Driscoll, Jeremy. "Evagrius and Paphnutius on the causes for abandonment by God." *Studia Monastica* 39.2 (1997): 259–86.

Elm, Suzanna. "Evagrius Ponticus' *Sententiae ad Virginem*." *Dumbarton Oaks Papers* 45 (1991): 265–95.

Evagrius of Pontus. *De diversis malignis cogitationibus*. PG 79.

―――. *Gnostikos*, ed. Antoine Guillaumont, *Évagre le Pontique: Le Gnostique ou a celui qui est devenu digne de la science*. SC 356; Paris: Cerf, 1989.

―――. *De jejunio*, ed. and trans. J. Muyldermans, *Evagriana Syriaca: Textes inédits du British Museum et de la Vaticane*. Louvain: Publications Universitaires/Institut Orientaliste, 1952.

―――. "Letter to Melania," trans. Martin Parmentier, "Evagrius of Pontus' 'Letter to Melania.'" *Bijdragen, tijdschrift voor filosofie en theologie* 46 (1985): 2–38.

―――. *Praktikos*, ed. A. and C. Guillaumont, *Évagre le Pontique: Traité pratique ou le moine*. SC 170–71; Paris: Cerf, 1971.

―――. *The Praktikos [and] Chapters on Prayer*, trans. John Eudes Bamberger. Kalamazoo: Cistercian, 1981.

―――. *Scholia on Ecclesiastes*, ed Paul Géhin, *Évagre le Pontique: Scholies à l'Ecclésiaste*. SC 397; Paris: Cerf, 1993.

―――. *Scholia on Proverbs*, ed Paul Géhin, *Évagre le Pontique: Scholies aux Proverbes*. SC 340; Paris: Cerf, 1987.

Evelyn White, Hugh G., ed. Walter Hauser. *The Monasteries of the Wâdi 'n Natrûn*. 3 vols.; New York: Metropolitan Museum of Art, 1926–1933 (repr. Arno Press: New York, 1973). Part I: *New Coptic Texts from the Monastery of Saint Macarius*; Part II: *The History of the Monasteries of Nitria and Scetis*; Part III: *The Architecture and Archaeology*.

Festugière, A.-J. *Sainte Thècle, Saints Côme et Damien, Saints Cyr et Jean (extraits), Saint Georges*. Paris, 1971.

Florovsky, Georges. "Theophilus of Alexandria and Apa Aphou of Pemdje," in *Harry Austryn Wolfson Jubilee Volume* (Jerusalem: American Academy for Jewish Research, 1965), I: 275–310; repr. in Georges Florovsky, *Collected Works*, vol. 4, *Aspects of Church History* (Belmont, Mass.: Nordland, 1975): 97–129.

Frankfurter, David. *Religion in Roman Egypt: Assimilation and Resistance.* Princeton: Princeton University Press, 1998.

Gendle, Nicholas. "Cappadocian elements in the mystical theology of Evagrius Ponticus." *Studia Patristica* 16: 373–84.

Goehring, James E. *Ascetics, Society, and the Desert: Studies in Early Egyptian Monasticism.* Studies in Antiquity and Christianity; Harrisburg, Pa.: Trinity, 1999.

Gould, Graham. *The Desert Fathers on Monastic Community.* Oxford: Clarendon, 1993.

―――. "The Image of God and the Anthropomorphite Controversy in Fourth Century Monasticism," in Robert J. Daley, ed., *Origeniana Quinta,* 549–65. Leuven: University Press, 1992.

Grossmann, Peter. "The Pilgrimage Center of Abû Mînâ," in David Frankfurter, ed., *Pilgrimage and Holy Space in Late Antique Egypt,* 281–302. Leiden: Brill, 1998.

Guillaumont, Antoine. *Les "Kephalaia Gnostica" d'Évagre le Pontique et l'histoire de l'origénisme chez les Grecs et chez les Syriens.* Patristica Sorboniensia, 5; Paris, 1962.

―――. *Aux origines du monachisme chrétien.* Spiritualité Orientale, 30; Solesmes: Bellefontaine, 1979.

―――. "L'Enseignement spirituel des moines d'Égypte," repr. in his *Études sur la spiritualité de l'orient chrétien,* 81–92. Bégrolles-en-Mauges: Bellefontaine, 1996.

―――. "The Jesus Prayer Among the Monks of Egypt." *Eastern Churches Review* 6 (1974): 66–71.

―――. "Le problème des deux Macaires dans les *Apophthegmata Patrum.*" *Irénikon* 48 (1975): 41–59.

―――. "Macarius the Egyptian, Saint," *The Coptic Encyclopedia,* ed. Aziz S. Atiya, 5.1491. New York: Doubleday, 1991.

Guy, Jean-Claude, ed. *Les Apophtegmes des Pères: Collection systématique. Chapitres I–IX.* SC 387; Paris: Cerf, 1993.

Hanson, R. P. C. *The Search for the Christian Doctrine of God.* Edinburgh: T & T Clark, 1988.

Harvey, Jr., Paul B., trans. "Jerome: Life of Paul, the First Hermit," in Vincent L. Wimbush, ed., *Ascetic Behavior in Greco-Roman Antiquity: A Sourcebook,* 357–69. Minneapolis: Fortress, 1990.

Heussi, Karl. *Der Ursprung des Mönchtums.* Tübingen, 1936.

Judge, E. A. "The Earliest Use of Monachos for 'Monk' (P. Coll. Youtie 77) and the Origins of Monasticism." *Jahrbuch für Antike und Christentum* 20 (1977): 72–89.

Kelly, J. N. D. *Early Christian Creeds.* London: Longmans, 1950.

———. *Golden Mouth: The Story of John Chrysostom.* Ithaca: Cornell University Press, 1995.

Kraus, J. "Hierakas." *Lexikon für Theologie und Kirche*, 5.321. 2nd ed.; Freiburg, 1957.

Lampe, G. W. H. *A Patristic Greek Lexicon.* Oxford: Clarendon, 1961.

Layton, Bentley. "Social Structure and Food Consumption in an Early Christian Monastery: The Evidence of Shenoute's Canons and the White Monastery Federation A.D. 385–465." *Le Muséon*, 115.1–2 (2002): 25–57.

Lohse, Bernhard. *Askese und Mönchtum in der Anrike und in der alten Kirche.* Munich, 1969.

Meinardus, Otto F.A. *Monks and Monasteries of the Egyptian Deserts.* Rev. ed.; Cairo: AUC Press, 1992.

el-Meskeen, Matta. *Coptic Monasticism and the Monastery of St. Macarius: A Short History.* Cairo: the Monastery of St Macarius, 1984.

Mikhail, Maged S., and Tim Vivian, trans. "Life of Saint John the Little." *Coptic Church Review* 18.1–2 (1997): 3–64.

Molinier, Nicolas. *Ascèse, contemplation et ministère d'après l'Histoire Lausiaque de Pallade d'Hélénopolis.* Spiritualité orientale 64; Bégrolles-en-Mauges: Bellefontaine, 1995.

Moschus, John. *Pratum spirituale. The Spiritual Meadow of John Moschus*, trans. John Wortley. Kalamazoo: Cistercian, 1992.

Müller, Liguori G. *The De Haeresibus of Saint Augustine.* Washington, D.C.: The Catholic University of America Press, 1956.

Murphy, Francis X. *Rufinus of Aquileia (345–411): His Life and Works.* Washington, D.C.: Catholic University of America Press, 1945.

———. "Melania the Elder: A Biographical Note," *Traditio* 5 (1947): 59–77.

———. "Evagrius Ponticus and Origenism," in Richard Hanson and Henri Crouzel, eds., *Origeniana Tertia*, 253–69. Rome: Edizioni dell' Ateneo, 1985.

Muyldermans, Joseph. "Evagriana Coptica." *Le Muséon* 76 (1963): 271–76.

O'Laughlin, Michael. "Origenism in the Desert." Th.D. Thesis, Harvard University, 1987.

_____. "The Anthropology of Evagrius Ponticus and its Sources," in C. Kannengiesser and W. Petersen, eds., *Origen of Alexandria: His World and His Legacy*, 357–73. Notre Dame: Univ. of Notre Dame Press, 1988.

Orban, Myriam, ed. *Déserts chrétiens d'Égypte*. Nice: Culture Sud, 1993.

Palladius. *Dialogus de vita S. Joannis Chrysostomi*, ed. P. R. Coleman-Norton. Cambridge: Cambridge University Press, 1928.

_____. *Palladius: Dialogue on the Life of St. John Chrysostom*, trans. Robert T. Meyer. Ancient Christian Writers, 45; New York and Mahwah: Newman, 1985.

_____. *The Lausiac History of Palladius*, ed. and trans. Cuthbert Butler. 2 vols.; Cambridge: Cambridge University Press, 1898 and 1904.

_____. *The Lausiac History*, ed. G. J. M. Bartelink, *Palladio: La Storia Lausiaca*. Milan: Fondazione Lorenzo Valla, 1974.

_____. *The Lausiac History*, trans. Robert T. Meyer. Ancient Christian Writers 34; New York: Newman, 1965.

Papini, Lucia, and David Frankfurter. "Fragments of the *Sortes Sanctorum* from the Shrine of St. Colluthus," in Frankfurter, ed., *Pilgrimage and Holy Space in Late Antique Egypt*, 393–401. Leiden: Brill, 1998.

Rahlfs, Alfred, ed. *Septuaginta*. Stuttgart: Deutsche Bibelstiftung Stuttgart, 1935.

Regnault, Lucien. *Les Sentences des Pères du désert: Troisieme recueil et tables*. Solesmes, Bellefontaine, 1976.

_____. *Les Sentences des pères du désert: série des anonymes*. Solesmes: Bellefontaine, 1985.

_____. *La vie quotidienne des pères du désert en Égypte au IVe siècle*. Paris: Hachette, 1990. Eng. trans. *The Day-to-Day Life of the Desert Fathers in Fourth-Century Egypt*. Petersham, Mass.: Saint Bede's, 1999.

_____. "Quelques apophthegmes arabes sur la 'Prière de Jésus,'" *Irénikon* 52 (1979): 344–55.

_____. "La prière continuelle 'monologistos' dans la littérature apophtegmatique." *Irénikon* 47 (1974): 467–93. Reprinted in *Les Pères du désert à travers leur Apophtegmes*, 113–39. Solesmes, 1987.

Russell, Norman, trans. *The Lives of the Desert Fathers: The Historia Monachorum in Aegypto*. Kalamazoo: Cistercian, 1980.

Solari, Placid. "Christ as Virtue in Didymus the Blind," in Harriet A. Luckman and Linda Kulzer, eds., *Purity of Heart in Early Ascetic and Monastic Literature*, 67–88. Collegeville: Liturgical Press, 1999.

Stewart, Columba. "Radical Honesty about the Self: the Practice of the Desert Fathers." *Sobornost* 12 (1990): 25–39.

———. "Feature Review: Three Recent Studies on Ancient Monasticism." *American Benedictine Review* 50.1 (1999): 3–11.

———. "Imageless Prayer and the Theological Vision of Evagrius Ponticus." *Journal of Early Christian Studies* 9:2 (2001): 173–204.

Strothmann, Werner, ed. *Die syrische Überlieferung der Schriften des Makarios.* 2 vols.; Wiesbaden: Harrossowitz, 1981.

Swanson, Mark N. " 'These Three Words Will Suffice': The 'Jesus Prayer' in Coptic Tradition," *Parole de l'Orient* 25 (2000): 695–714.

Theodoret. *Religious History,* trans. R. M. Price, *A History of the Monks of Syria.* Kalamazoo: Cistercian, 1985.

Timbie, Janet. "A Liturgical Procession in the Desert of Apa Shenoute," in David Frankfurter, ed., *Pilgrimage and Holy Space in Late Antique Egypt,* 415–41. Leiden: Brill, 1998.

Toda, Satoshi. "La Vie de S. Macaire l'Égyptien: État de la question." *Analecta Bollandiana* 118:3–4 (2000): 267–90.

Turner, C. H. "Palladiana II: The Lausiac History. Questions of History." *Journal of Theological Studies* 22 (1921): 21–35, 138–55.

van Esbroeck, Michel. "La dormition chez les coptes," *Actes du IVe Congrès Copte, Louvain-la-Neuve, 5–10 sept. 1988,* ed. M. Rassart-Debergh et J. Ries, 436–45. Publications de l'Institut Orientaliste de Louvain 41; Louvain-la-Neuve: Institut Orientaliste, 1992. Repr. in van Esbroeck, *Aux origines de la Dormition de la Vierge: Etudes historiques sur les traditions orientales,* XI. 436–45. Collected Studies Series 472; Aldershot: Variorum, 1995.

Veilleux, Armand, ed., *Pachomian Koinonia.* Kalamazoo: Cistercian, 1980.

Vivian, Tim. *Paphnutius: Histories of the Monks of Upper Egypt and the life of Onnophrius.* Kalamazoo: Cistercian, 1993.

———. *Journeying into God.* Minneapolis: Fortress, 1996.

———. "Words to Live By: 'A Conversation that the Elders Had with One Another Concerning Thoughts (ΠΕΡΙ ΛΟΓΙΣΜΩΝ).' " *St. Vladimir's Theological Quarterly* 39:2 (1995): 127–41.

———. "The Good God, the Holy Power, and the Paraclete: 'To the Sons of God' (*Ad filios Dei*) by Saint Macarius the Great." *Anglican Theological Review* 30.3 (1998): 338–65.

_____. "The Monasteries of the Wadi Natrun, Egypt: A Personal and Monastic Journey." *American Benedictine Review* 49:1 (March 1998): 3–32.

Vivian, Tim, and Apostolos N. Athanassakis, trans., *The Life of Saint George of Choziba.* San Francisco: ISP, 1994.

_____. *The Life of Antony.* Kalamazoo: Cistercian, 2003.

Vivian, Tim, and Birger A. Pearson. "Saint Paul of Tamma on the Monastic Cell (de Cella)," *Hallel* 23.2 (1998): 86–107.

Vogt, Kari. "The Coptic Practice of the Jesus Prayer: A Tradition Revived," 111–20 in Nelly Van Doorn-Harder and Kari Vogt, eds., *Between Desert and City: The Coptic Orthodox Church Today.* Oslo: Novus forlag, 1997.

Vogüé, Adalbert de. "Les fragments coptes de l'Histoire Lausiaque: l'édition d'Amélineau et le manuscrit." *Orientalia* 58.3 (1989): 326–32.

_____. "La version copte du chapitre XVII de l'Histoire Lausiaque: Les deux éditeurs et les trois manuscrits." *Orientalia* 58.4 (1989): 510–24.

_____. "Le texte copte du chapitre XVIII de l'Histoire Lausiaque: L'édition d'Amélineau et le manuscrit." *Orientalia* 61.4 (1992): 459–62.

Ward, Benedicta, trans. *The Sayings of the Desert Fathers: The Alphabetical Collection.* Rev. ed.; Kalamazoo: Cistercian, 1984.

Ware, Kallistos. "The Origins of the Jesus Prayer: Diadochus, Gaza, Sinai," in Cheslyn Jones, Geoffrey Wainwright, Edward Yarnold, eds., *The Study of Spirituality* 175–184. New York: Oxford University Press, 1986.

Williams, Rowan. *The Wound of Knowledge: Christian Spirituality from the New Testament to St. John of the Cross.* Cambridge, Mass.: Cowley, 1991.

POPULAR PATRISTICS SERIES

ST VLADIMIR'S SEMINARY PRESS
1-800-204-2665 • www.svspress.com